Films, Poems, Codes

46 Film Proposals, Collected Poems 1968–2017, and New Torah Code Findings

Original Film Treatments by the Author,
Poems (some published in 5 countries),
and Torah Code Findings
Not Previously Published

Steve Canada

Author of:

(1) Bible-Encoded Crop Circle Gods (4 alien mysteries solved).

(2) Foretold in Sacred Code (all of history found encoded in the Torah).

(3) Death's Bible Code (accidents, assassinations, holocaust, mass shootings, natural disasters, terror attacks, wars – shown in Torah Matrices).

(4) End of Days 2014-2018 (adjusted Gregorian Calendar shows timeframe).

(5) Heaven and Hell Are Full, Angels of All Religions Returning at End of Days, AD 2014-2018 – Names Shown in Torah Matrices.

(6) Celebrities and Movie Stars Death Bible Code, Vol.1: Their Deadly Diseases and Names Shown in Torah Matrices.

(7) Celebrities and Movie Stars Death Bible Code, Vol.2: Their Fatal Cancers and Names Shown in Torah Matrices.

(8) Celebrities and Movie Stars Death Bible Code, Vol.3: Their Deaths by Accidents, Murders, Overdoses, and Suicides … and Names Shown in Torah Matrices.

(9) Event Code Uncovered – Secrets Buried in Sacred Text. More Historical Events Revealed Encoded in the Hebrew Torah.

authorHOUSE®

AuthorHouse™
1663 Liberty Drive
Bloomington, IN 47403
www.authorhouse.com
Phone: 1 (800) 839-8640

Published by AuthorHouse 04/28/2017

ISBN: 978-1-5246-8908-7 (sc)
ISBN: 978-1-5246-8907-0 (e)

Library of Congress Control Number: 2017906270

Print information available on the last page.

CONTENTS

LIST OF ILLUSTRATIONS

In Book 3: New Bible Code Findings

Book 1

FILMS

INTRODUCTION

Some of these 46 film treatments could be in script development by publication date of this book. The author is open to negotiation from producers and agents. One such film idea ("Election Repair") shows how the Democrats could win the U.S. presidency perpetually from now on. My degrees in Sociology has helped me have insights into a type of social engineering – applied to problem-solving, in this case national election results and how one party could guarantee dominance for many generations. More of the inevitable conflict and intrigue come when the counter-moves by the Republicans are considered, adding to the drama of the complicated possibilities.

LIST OF 46 FILM TREATMENTS AND PROPOSALS, TITLES AND GENRES:

"Turnabout," thriller
"Timeyons," scifi
"Airbag," suspense
"Atonement," scifi
"Avenging Angels Return to Earth at End of Days," scifi
"The Bible Code Murders," thriller
"Dark Moon Defense," scifi
"Defeating Drought – Moving Water," drama
"Defeating Hurricanes," drama-adventure
"Dome Houses," drama
"Helmet," suspense
"Hollywood Deaths Foretold," drama, mystery, thriller
"Iceberg Solution – Drought Buster," drama
"Jihad Comfort," terrorism thriller
"Killing Tornadoes," thriller-adventure

"Peace (Chem) Trails," drama-mystery

"Plane Crashes Bible-Code Predicted – Airline Deaths Foretold," mystery-thriller

"Secede!," political thriller

"Secret Mission to Olam," scifi, alien contact thriller

"Terror Attack Deaths Foretold in Sacred Text," mystery-thriller

"Titanic's Destined Deaths," mystery, drama

"Volcano Code," adventure-mystery

"Assassination Code," political intrigue

"Beheadings Code," political thriller

"Car Crash Code," mystery

"Earthquake Code," adventure-mystery

"Fireproof Houses," thriller

"Genocide Code," mystery-adventure

"Holy Flood!," mystery-adventure

"Holy Landslide!," mystery-adventure

"Lower the Seas – Save the Planet," mystery, thriller, adventure

"Museum Immortal," drama-mystery

"Nuke Plant Meltdown Code," disaster thriller

"Predicting U.S. Presidents," political intrigue

"Saving Russia," historical political thriller

"School and Mass Shootings Code," mystery-thriller

"Store the Heat, Save the Planet," adventure political thriller

"Train Crash Code," political intrigue

"Tsunami Code," mystery-thriller

"War Deaths' Code," mystery-thriller

"WWII A-Bombs' Code," historical political thriller

"Dirty Bomb School Buses," terror thriller

"Election Repair: Hillary 2020 – How She Can Win," political drama

"Legal Ivory – Saving the Elephants," wildlife conservation

"Lahmu Denied (Mars Rebuke)," scifi thriller adventure

"The Life of Coins," children's animated film

PART 1: "TURNABOUT," FILM TREATMENT

Turnabout

written by

Stephen Andrew Canada

registered with the WGA, West (Hollywood, California)

Logline: College film crew barely escape with their lives from several foreign countries when they try to make a movie there similar to 'Brokeback Mountain,' portraying those nations' cultural iconic folk figures as homosexual.

Thesis: Since turnabout is fair play, making a movie in other countries along the lines of 'Brokeback Mountain' could prove to be a revealing cross-cultural study in tolerance and degrees of homophobia or acceptance of homosexuality, much less to what extent officials in those countries even allow such a movie be made, and even promoted and distributed.

ACT 1

ROGER ALLISON (45, Anglo, married, with a 20-year old daughter at college out of state), assistant head of the film department at a small Christian college in Tulsa, Oklahoma, holds a monthly party at his house for department faculty, staff, and grad-uate students.

Scene at one of those recent parties shows conversations among him and some fac-ulty and grad students about the subject of his film project idea of trying to make a version of 'Brokeback Mountain' in foreign countries other than English-speaking or Western European. "Is it possible? Would anyone in those countries object or resist its filming or distribution? A man from China came here and directed that Academy Award winning movie, so why couldn't we as foreigners go overseas and make a similar movie about *their* cultural icons?" Some see trouble ahead if he tries, and encourage him to pursue other film projects.

Assistant professor Allison, seeking tenure in the film department, applies for fun-ding for the project. The department resists his written proposal, but he finally convinces them to at least try. He gets approval to take three grad students with him, two males and one female:

JOHN CHANG McCARDY (adopted from North Korea as an infant orphan, now 23), a serious, dedicated graduate student.

BILL MONROE (blonde Nebraska farmboy, 24), who has a bi-side in the closet he's struggling with on several levels, not the least of which is parental,

SUSAN FAWNSKIN (Native American, Shawnee tribe, 24; her mother, Ravenhair, was married five times); she's not exactly 'curious yellow,' but is nudging herself in that direction one stray odor at a time, immobile as her heart has become on the hetero side,

NINA JEROME (replaces Susan in Act 3; black, 24, widow, mother of a 3-year-old girl; Air Force husband was killed while on guard patrol in Afghanistan).

Roger secures funding outside the college to supplement what little the film de-partment has budgeted for this graduate film project. Some of it on 'gofundme.com.' He has been struggling for tenure for several years now, causing tension in his marriage. This overseas filming project could carry the weight for the committee that finally puts his candidacy over the top. He doesn't want to be stuck on a dead-end teaching track, and has dreams of moving to a larger college, in another state.

Susan makes clear to the rest of the team (Roger, John, and Bill; mustering up her courage to mask her insecurity, she puts on a brave face) that while she is at the college because of affirmative action on the basis of her gender, and her minority racial status, and her Shawnee Native American tribal nation membership, she feels fully capable of contributing her fair share positively to the project, and is committed to its success.

Personality conflicts and group dynamics split the group into two factions, Roger and Susan against John and Bill, as they share their vision of the project. Roger ex-plains that they don't have to believe in the premise of the proposed film – a version of 'Brokeback Mountain' could not safely be made by foreigners in most of the world – but just need to make the movie and get it done as best they can.

Roger: "Brokeback Mountain was a short story that first appeared in The New Yorker October 13, 1997. As a 2005 Hollywood movie, it won awards all over the world, including Oscars for Best Director, Best Adapted Sceen - play, Best Drama Motion Picture, Best Director, and Best Screenplay."

Bill to Roger: "You realize this project is politically incorrect, don't you?"

Roger: "Only in the post-ironic sense of the French New Wave."

John, interrupting: "Yes, but still, how can you prove a negative?"

Roger: "Whaddya mean?"

John: "You say you believe such a movie can't be made in most countries, other than what is called the First World, where they're too decadent to even know wto protest or resist … but isn't that a kind of self-fulfilling prophesy?"

Roger: "I didn't make up the rules for what movies are made in other countries, so how could I control what they allow produced there or not?"

Susan: "You'll choose counties where it's obvious such a movie can't be made, like in Muslim countries, where they wouldn't allow it."

Roger: "I understand the potential bias you're talking about, so we could elimi-nate those obvious ones, leaving those for other film departments or production companies to tackle. So how about keeping it in just North America to start with? We'll try up in Canada, and then we'll try down in Mexico. The budget doesn't allow for air travel and hotels overseas for a group our size anyway."

ACT 2

They plan their trip north, fly to Ottawa, check into a hotel and contact a film casting office, prior to scouting locations around the city, after taking a tourist's bus tour of the city.

The major characters are to be two Mounties as subjects of the main plot. A new recruit is mentored by an officer, and their incendiary chemistry is the start of a long-standing affair they're careful to keep secret, since such liaisons are strictly against police policy and rules.

They learn too late that foreign filmmakers are required by Canadian law to register with the Canadian Film Board if they plan on making a movie in Canada. They've been followed and monitored by immigration agents since they exited the Ottawa airport. Suspicions were aroused when they told passport control they were scouting for a mo-vie shoot but were unclear exactly where they were interested in scouting or that they had not yet gotten clearance or approval from the Film Board.

They are surveilled and bugged by the Canadian National Police Special Projects Unit (CNPSPU, or SPU for short), but detect a tail only after they had scouted some possible sites and contacted a talent agency for interviews and casting. They change hotels and keep conversations in the room to a whisper, and in the hotel's restaurant talk only in general and oblique terms, trying to develop an *ad hoc* code that doesn't work very well at calming their nerves as they grow more and more apprehensive about trying to make this movie.

In the middle of the night, fearful of getting arrested, they pack up and leave the hotel, and take a train out of the province, westward toward Calgary, a cattle industry city in the south-central part of the country, and change their film focus to cowboys there.

Casting goes well, and they film two actors in a discreet relationship; nothing graphic or overt.

Female cowgirls are also performing at a rodeo there. Some are new to the circuit and look to the more experienced one to lead the way on what's best to do. Subtle attraction between two of the cowgirls lead to a warm, close and passionate affair. The fiance of one of them suspects something is going on but has no specific thing to go on. The irony of love creates a special suffering for those who can't resist the lure.

Susan and one of the cowgirls meet by accident, form a friendship, and they quickly fall in love. Susan decides to stay in Calgary with her new love. She plans to have her Tulsa roommate send her belongings from their apartment, and to finish her Master's degree with a paper for credit, after applying for residency in Alberta province.

Roger and Susan argue over her staying in Calgary with her new-found cowgirl girl-friend. A loud, angry confrontation in which Roger sincerely feels he's looking out for her best interests.

Susan: "I've Got to do this! I didn't know before that I wanted it, but now that I've found it, I can't leave. It would be wrong and stupid to leave."

> Roger: "How can you make a life here? How can you finish your degree from
> up here?"

> Susan: "I've got only two more papers due, and I'm assuming you'll give me
> credit for being part of this film project. I can research and write here and mail
> the papers in."

Roger: "Have you thought this through?"

Susan: "No, but what in life can be, thoroughly enough?"

Argument continues to resolution of Roger accepting her decision and promising his support. Becoming more paranoid from being followed, the team talks about how to protect their digital information, and if to use encryption or whether or not that would look suspicious.

Roger: "Yes, that might seem suspicious, but there's a way to email comp-letely securely and confidentially, with no way to intercept or detect."

Susan: "Without encryption? And encryption can be broken anyway, so there's no complete assurance there."

Roger: "Yes, all you need to know is the person's email address and password, for absolutely secure communication."

Bill: "And bypass any possible intercept? How's that possible?"

Roger: "The writer who wants his message read just saves it as a draft. Anyone who wants to read it, and who knows the addy and password, just goes into the account and clicks on Draft, and reads it."

John: "Why would that be secure and private?"

Roger explains in detail how it works, step by step.

Susan packs and says emotional goodbyes to the group and leaves the hotel to join her new friend. The remaining three team members suspect the Film Board or the police are closing in on them, so they too pack quickly and slip out of the hotel to the bus station, and take a bus south across the border, then make bus connections back to Tulsa and the college.

ACT 3

At the college a replacement for Susan is recruited, a female black grad student also in the film department, NINA JEROME, 24, widow, mother of a little girl, age 3, who is cared for by grandparents when Nina is away. Her husband was in the Air Force, and killed while on guard patrol in Afghanistan.

Funding for the Mexico part of the project is secured, a car is rented and they drive south across Texas to Juarez, Mexico, stopping for the night and seeing the sights. Then south to Saltillo in the state of Coahilla, north of Monterrey.

Using a local casting agency, they start rehearsing and filming at several scouted sites. One of the Mexican cowboys is also a bullfighter. Bill and he hit it off as friends.

The team is detained by Mexican police and Roger is interrogated in a restrained and threatening way, with undertones of implied violence to come. They manage to escape due to lack of the guards' attention.

Making their way around town down some alleys at night, they are assaulted and robbed. They'd hidden some credit cards in their shoes and use them to buy bus tickets after checking out of the hotel.

While packing to leave, Bill informs the group he plans to stay behind with the bull-fighter he met on the set. They try to argue him out of it but he's adamant and has made up his mind, explaining he'll deal with the immigration problem when it comes up, but will apply for residency right away, maybe on the basis of a student visa to begin with.

> Roger: (taking Bill aside; in a confidential and caring tone): "What brought this on?"
>
> Bill: "It snuck up on me and hit me me like a ton of bricks. I had a couple of brief encounters as a teenager but always thought of them as adolescent experimentation. I never thought I'd have another, but this is different, it's overwhelming and pure and real. All of a sudden I felt committed, and can't see myself going on without him."
>
> Roger: "What will you do, just stay here with him? How will you survive?"
>
> Bill: "He has a place to live, and a decent income. He's offered to share everything with me. And if I can find some kind of work, we can make a real go of it. I never knew I could feel like this. I've got to give it a try Bill, I really do."

The rest of the remaining team, Roger, Nina and John, board a bus heading north. It's full, with luggage on the roof, and some peasants carrying cages of live chickens. After about forty miles the bus breaks down. They gather their luggage and walk to the nearest town, about two miles north, and buy train tickets. Their tickets are for almost the last available seats.

The whole train is full of mothers and their Zika babies, infants born with small heads – mothers from South and Central America, and Mexico, a train organized by the Mexican government. The news had spread of U.S. policy to care for such children, and President Obama allocating emergency funds of over a billion dollars to develop a vaccine.

Roger asks John and Nina to take out the video camera and sound boom, while he asks the passengers quietly and gently, in Spanish, in turn for their permission to film them for a documentary that could create more interest in caring for their children. He just hopes he can get the footage past the U.S. Border Patrol.

-- FADE OUT –

EPILOGUE

Roger's press release, "Attempted Remake in Two Foreign Countries of 'Brokeback Mountain' a Disaster," about his attempts to make a version of that movie in Canada (RMP, cowboys, and cowgirls) and in Mexico (gauchos, and bullfighters) that got the crew arrested, detained, interrogated, fined, and chased out of those countries, drew such attention that other film departments and production companies saw it as a challenge for them to go overseas and try and make a version of it themselves.

'Brokeback Mountain' had a very particular target, a carefully constructed cultural artifact for deeper impact on a national psyche, an essential part of a society's identity, the archetypal folk hero … in that case, the American cowboy.

The argument was that not in ONE other nation other than the USA would it be tolerated to depict such a folk hero iconic embodiment of national tradition and character as homosexual. The erstwhile filmmakers would be denied permission to film, harassed, criticized, attacked, arrested, tortured, then deported (if they didn't die at the hands of their torturers and executioners).

Attempts by studios large and small spread. The popularity of the effort across the film industry to try and make a 'Brokeback Mountain' movie overseas became some-what of a *cause celebre*, but the cost in lives finally did put an end to the campaign, even among the most independent and rebel filmmakers. They didn't want to give up, but the body-count mounted and the public outcry and shareholders' objections were finally too much for the studio execs to resist.

Organizing the effort as an undercover operation as a way to skirt governmental monitoring and interference helped to some extent. Security and surveillance expertise was enlisted to enhance the likelihood of successfully completing this movie in the in-tended home countries. Countermeasures were employed to get around government tracking.

Other officials are cultured and sophisticated in their objections to Americans com-ing to their country and attempting to demean its heritage and traditions. Some officials allow partial development of the film to go forward, knowing that at some point they'd intervene and arrest the group of arrogant interlopers, having then more evidence on which charges could be based, could be gathered and prosecution more likely successful, hopefully with long prison sentences for all of them.

Close calls send the message to powers-that-be of impending sanctions that could spell the end of fun and games and business as usual. No matter how hard they tried, they could not break through the resistance of getting this movie made anywhere over-seas. There are over 200 countries in the world, so there is no shortage of locations to choose from.

Iran did not disappoint in its predilection to take Americans hostage. The crew was charged with anti-Islam conspiracy and anti-Republic plans to defame its heritage and customs, and imprisoned them in the infamous Evan prison in Tehran. Later, prisoner swap negotiations began, further humiliating Washington and the White House.

In each country where the crew was able to escape, the visit ends with a narrow, harrowing getaway when they are able to evade capture. They got away by a variety of means, by train, auto, by foot, by air, and by boat, running from threats of death, with gunfire in heavy traffic of high-speed car chases. Each segment also featured a country as partial travelogue too, with some cultural history, along with food, and art history, and music.

If they are not killed, they are chased out of every single country where they try to arrange filming this movie, by those protective enough of their folk heroes and cultural traditions to take seriously an attempt, especially by foreigners, to insult them.

In Chile, portraying the *huaso,* they run for their lives across the mountains to Argentina.

In Argentina, portraying *gauchos*, they barely escape with their lives.

In Brazil, portraying soccer players, they're tortured (a member dies), then are deported.

In Syria, the crew was lined up against a wall and shot. A clear enough message for anyone to get. President Assad and his Iranian and Russian backers are blunt about it.

In Ethiopia, all members of the crew were stoned to death.

In Chad, they were buried alive.

In Nigeria, they were hanged.

In Egypt, they were shot by firing squad.

In Uzbekistan, they were beheaded.

In Japan (portraying Samurai, and also Sumo wrestlers in their movie), they were gutted by the Yakuza and left to die in a rice paddy. Rice paddies in Japan are still to-day fertilized by human feces (the author can attest to this fact personally, at least as of the late 1940s, having slipped and ridden his bicycle into one totally by accident as a child of about age eight. The hose washing-off on the porch by his mother was no fun).

In Turkistan, they were tortured to death.

In Iraq, they were captured by a gang of teens, moved westward, and sold to ISIL; and are still captives. Secret talks are underway for purchase of their release.

In Indonesia, they were boiled alive in the jungle, then roasted on a spit and eaten.

In Russia, they were dissolved in a vat of acid by the Russian Mob.

In Kazakhstan, they were beheaded and their bodies fed to wild dogs.

In Pakistan, they were raped and sodomized til dead.

In Afghanistan, they were skinned alive and left for wild animals to eat.

In India, they were burnt in a large furnace.

In South Korea, they were drowned in a rice paddy and their bodies thrown over the border into North Korea.

In Congo, they were burned at the stake.

In Libya, they were beheaded, their bodies buried in the desert and their heads thrown out to sea, to float and bob on currents north to Europe.

In Sicily, they were drawn and quartered, pulled apart by horses.

In Vietnam, they were tied standing over fast-growing bamboo plants that grew up through their intestines.

In Sudan, they were staked spread-eagle on the ground, sprinkled with honey, and eaten alive by fire ants and stung by scorpions.

In Yemen, they were crucified on large wooden crosses, placed in a row along a main road out of the capital, Sana'a. A lesson for all infidels.

In Somalia, the crew was crucified, the crosses lined up in a row along a major road to the capital. Koranic justifications were pinned to their chests.

Recommendation: do not try to make this movie anywhere but in the USA, or maybe a few other English-speaking countries, or a few countries in northern Europe. Otherwise, it's a suicide mission.

Addendum to Epilogue: Challenge to all filmmakers – go overseas to any non-West-ern country and try to make a 'Brokeback Mountain-like' movie in which the society's essential iconic figures or folk heroes are depicted as gay. Then promote it generously and distribute it widely in-country, and see how much notoriety, recognition, and how many awards it receives. Unfortunately, too many filmmakers did take up the challenge, and got themselves in more trouble than they were prepared to handle, with deadly consequences for the crews. When we naively project our liberal, Progressive views of tolerance onto other societies, we are rudely surprised when they are willing to defend their core cultural values. Some call that intolerance. They might call it survival through protection and preservation. Some call that conservative, even reactionary. No one said you couldn't have a good time as your culture decays around you. The decline of civilization had been going on a long time. That doesn't preclude you from enjoying the ride. While despair for the West might be warranted, giving up the fight too soon might not be advised in any event. A renewal and renaissance in a new direction could be developing, one healthy for the culture and its supporting institutions.

THE END –

'Timeyons' (particles of time), Film Treatment, partial film script, March-April 2016,
by Steve Canada

1   Logline, Pitch, Description
2   Synopsis
3   Outline
4   Treatment

Logline: Astronomer Catherine Shoste (blonde, 35, Jodie Foster-like figure in Carl Sagan's 'Contact') detects disintegration of space and time at edges of the far universe, a process that allows detection for the first time separate particles of time. She designates them 'Timeyons,' and organizes a team to create anti-time particles and beam them in all directions, to hopefully slow and stop the universe's collapse.

Pitch: 'Contact' meets 'Oblivion,' meets potential Apocalypse.

Description: A cosmology disaster drama of scientists struggling to reverse the collapse of the universe, using the new discovery of time particles, following the recent detection of gravitational waves on September 14, 2015. Given the 100-year old Einstein theory of General Relativity, that predicted gravity waves, this is no coincidence, since space and gravity are intimately related, and space-time is integral to the fabric of existence. The key to saving the universe is to somehow counter the imploding hypersphere using beams of anti-time particles.

Synopsis: Inter-agency politics almost derail her efforts. After much struggle and frust-rating dead-ends and delays, the Beam Team finally succeeds in preserving parts of the cosmos from collapse, although new realities call for some of physics and the notion of time to be fundamentally revised.

Alien contact is detected in some of the recorded signals from the far reaches of space, providing hope for reconnection with ancient astronauts known to the Sumerians as Anunnaki, about 5000 years ago. The Sumerians, the first human civilization, knew them as their leaders and teachers, who came to Earth about 450,000 years ago, in search of gold, from the solar system's ninth planet, Nibiru.

The crumbling of space-time at the universe's far reaches had an energy signature differential detected in a narrow part of the infrared band range, found in the Hubble telescope data. This was verified by other team members and correlated by major telescopes around the world.

Their discussions are monitored by the NSA, and reported to the Pentagon once some of the implications are realized. To avoid public panic, all information on the discovery is classified and personnel sworn to secrecy and detained in facilities at their labs in an international effort to avoid leaks and geopolitical enemies taking advantage of potential social and economic chaos.

If the story gets out, how will the media handle it, and how will humanity face its prospective demise? Does a segment suspect a plot to scare enough people so they'll accept a law-and order crack-down, or even martial law? Who's telling the truth and who can be trusted? How fast will the story be distorted in a social media and fake-news world? How much will such inevitable distortions contribute to or even help cause public unrest and the breakdown of social, political and economic order?

As the universe collapses at an unknown rate – unknown because impinging time particles are distorting local time readings – potential destruction closes in from all directions. The collapse rate of the hypersphere is unknown, and involves complex ratios of gravity, energy and light, the measured values all of which keep changing unpredictably.

While the forces of nature had been discrete and constant til now, they fluctuate in surprising ways, as if new voices were composing an unwritten operetta for a new soprano.

Outline:

Act 1: opening scene – extreme edge of universe, with frying sound as particles of time bubble up and separate from the fabric of space – tiny sparks flying away from the space curvature.

Cut to: astronomical observatory where Catherine Shoste and her assistant, Tony Heglund (Nordic good looks, 30) have first inkling of detecting an anomaly in the farthest reaches of space (pp.1-3 of dialogue).

Cut to: other research locations, with personnel, dialogue pp.4-9.

Cut to: Keck observatory in Hawaii (pp.10-12 of dialogue) –

"When the universe stops expanding and starts collapsing, the reverse entropy will create a new history. The end point of the future will stop progressing, and time running backward will need to account for an unknown past since the collapse of space involves new, random and unique events that won't duplicate our known past, but will create new past events unknown on the timeline of our history."

"Yes, that unfolding will be as unique as the future created as the universe was exploding in an entropic universe with its one-way arrow of time. The reverse arrow of backward time will track a collapse, an anti-entropic energy organization of a new reality that creates its own future as a new past, a new history that un-writes itself even before it blooms forth."

"How long will the universe exist? Come with me to the end of time, and I will show you."

"Dial up Now on your Rolodex and we can adjust the frequency of brain tissue to slow perception of the time variable."

"That amounts to a joke in the mind-body problem, a conundrum Nature is still trying to figure out. So don't be fooled by its tricks, or its illusions."

Cut to: NSA personnel at signal monitoring terminals (pp.13-17 of dialogue).

Act 2:

Scene at: Berkeley Linear Accelerator (dialogue pp.1-4).
Scene at: CERN, on France-Swiss border (dialogue p. 5).
Scene at: FBI Special Projects Group (dialogue pp.6-7)
Scene at: Two Beam Team members walking outside and talking (dialog pp. 8-10).
Scene at: NSA in safe room, two group heads talking (dialogue pp.11-15).
Scene at: White House, with Catherine (dialogue p. 16).

Act 3:

    Scene at: Berkeley Linear Accelerator (dialogue pp.1-2).
    Scene at: NSA, two weeks later; two scientists (dialogue pp.3-4).
    Scene at: White House (dialogue pp.5-7).
    Scene at: Beam Team Control Room (dialogue p.8).

Epilogue: voice over (2 pp. of text).

THE END

PART 2: 19 FILM QUERY-PROPOSALS SENT TO AGENTS (EXCEPT AIRBAG, HELMET, & SECEDE!):

<u>From</u>: Steve Canada [see my 30 books, on Amazon, Books-in-Print, Author House, etc.; Google my name, as author, to see titles].
<u>RE</u>: screenwriter looking for representation

Dear Manager,

I am a writer working on a full length screenplay that I believe your agency may be interested in representing. Please find a short pitch below for your review.

<u>Title</u>: AIRBAG

<u>Genre</u>: Suspense

<u>Log Line</u>: The real reason shrapnel is part of the Takata airbag design goes back to Aug. 9, 1945, Nagasaki, Japan, where relatives of the corporation's executives died from the A-bomb.

<u>Pitch</u>: Revenge may be sweet, but it's also ugly, especially when it's bloody, disfiguring and deadly. Pay-back for the Nagasaki A-bomb by relatives who died there who work for the Takata Corp., the largest auto airbag manufacturer in the world, explains the so-called "design flaw" that has killed and injured thousands in the U.S. alone.

<u>Description</u>: Some of the Takata Corp. executives' family members were among those 70 thousand incinerated and vaporized near ground zero in Nagasaki on August 9, 1945. Beyond ancestor worship, revenging dead relatives who no longer have any chance to defend themselves; obligatory in the Shinto view of life and set of ancient values.

Plausible deniability was part of the plan to kill, wound and disfigure as many people as possible in America. No one could, based on verifiable, traceable evidence, connect the "design flaw" back to the Takata executives. They had taken a blood oath in the Samurai tradition.

"You'll notice there have been no *hari kari* committed over this shame. What does that tell you?"

"It tells me there is no shame in authentic vengeance, which would never be apologized for in that ancient tradition."...

"Are you claiming it's just an undetected design defect, or perhaps only a minor flaw in the manufacturing process? How naive can you be?"

"You've made up your mind before examining all the evidence!"

"I've seen the shredded faces of beautiful white women across America. That's enough evidence for me."

"At least in early January 2017 Takata pleaded guilty in federal court, and paid the one billion dollar fine. Eleven people have died from the shrapnel projected into the vehicles' cabins."

"You and I know that's not enough punishment. Pleading in court and paying some of their enormous worldwide profits as blood money doesn't begin to match the enormity of their crimes or come close to what they deserve."

"There's got to be another way to get at them."

If this has piqued your interest, I could send you a hardcopy of the screenplay's Synopsis, Outline, and/or short Treatment for your consideration. Then, if you like those, we could discuss sending the script.

Thanks, Steve Canada

<u>SASE enclosed for return of these pages if no interest.</u>

Other than these 3 queries, I'm working on about 36 other film ideas, all in various stages of script development. Might you want to see more of my queries? Can yousee this as made for tv movie?

From: Steve Canada
RE: screenwriter looking for representation

Dear Manager,

I am a writer working on a feature length screenplay that I believe your agencymay be interested in representing. Please find a short pitch below for your review.

Title: ATONEMENT

Genre: Sci-fi

Logline: Love trumps desire for greatly extended lifespan – an interplanetary love story.

Pitch: An Anunnaki left behind by mistake upon departure of the final members of the Ruling Council of 12 and their staff from the Nazca Plain in about year 1100 finds love and chooses the love of a human woman over extended life (endemic to his genome, if special elixirs are provided).

Description: Upon the departure from Earth of the last of the Anunnaki, from the Nazca Plain of Peru, in about year 1100, one by mistake is left behind. In the tension, stress and confusion of the final departure from their 'Home in the Faraway,' Eridu [Earth], he is late, and overlooked. He comes to reconcile with his fate and accepts his shortened life expectancy and inevitable death as he learns to love in the context of risk and commitment. He gives up a chance at immortality for the complex love of a human woman.

He opts for mortal love and an earlier death than would be expected in his kind.Lack of special nutrient supplements and gene therapies will allow his telomeres to to shorten with each cell replacement, ensuring his hastened demise and eventual shortened lifespan from tens of thousands of years to hundreds.

SCENE: conversation between his wife and him –
"You just like to lord it over us, that you live forever and we don't!"
"We just live more years than you, not forever. And without the elixirs, my aging will accelerate, and death at some point will be inevitable."
"They might return and save you, rescue you, and you'll want to leave me then!"
"No, it would not be allowed. And I never want to leave you."
"Could they take me with you if they come back to rescue you?"
"That also would not be allowed. And there is no rescue mission coming."
"How do you know?"
"Only king Anu can choose humans to ascend to Olam and that has not been done for a very long time, not since Elijah. I think king Anu learned his lesson – it did not turn out as well as expected."
"But you would go if they came back for you."

"I am sure they already sense I am committed to you and want to remain here, no matter the consequences. They would not expend the resources to try and convince me otherwise. I love you, and will not leave you."

(They hug and kiss; she feels deeply reassured).

How does he avoid detection and the wrath of the local authorities and the populace at large? If he was discovered and identified as an Anunnaki he would be detained and questioned, and imprisoned as a threat to the state.

He avoids discovery by adjusting his behavior to conform to cultural norms and expectations. As a trained anthropologist, he has observed and cataloged human behavior and practices for centuries. He prefers anonymity to standing out as exceptional, so tones down his displays of knowledge and abilities.

Inevitably, some of those he encounters grow suspicious at his uniqueness, perfection and gifts, but they learn to accept these as appealing natural endowments. Several times he has to back off from seeming to know too much, and never having physical complaints or ailments. To appear more normal, he pretends to forget certain things. Or not to know certain facts, and to have an occasion ache or pain. Asking for help with something minor also helped him to appear more normal.

As their relationship deepens and their mutual commitment strengthens. He gives an account of how he was left behind that makes her wonder if it had been intentional, either by them or by him *wanting* to remain and deceiving them by missing the deadline for departure. The true nature of his intentions is now questioned, and we wonder what his actual plans and motivation are.

The birth of their first child, a perfect daughter (what used to be called a demigod, the issue from a union between an Anunnaki and a human, who are themselves a hybrid, the result of the long-ago insemination of a female primate with the seed of an Anunnaki), doesn't go far enough for his wife to dispel all doubts about hismission here.

Scene on Nibiru; discussion by two members of the Supervisory Team:

A: "If there is a source for myths for the things that are, where does the truth of things that are to come *come* from? He is left behind."

B: "But he was able to accomplish his final task, that of securing the Ark of the Covenant from the Vatican. King Anu had deemed it essential for final removal. It had been stolen from the Hebrews long ago and stored deep beneath the pope's residence. It was a weapon given to the Hebrews by the Anunnaki, which assured their victory in battles and thus their survival. But for the long term, people could not be trusted with it."

A: "The decision has been made not to return or rescue him. What will be his story?"

B: "Isolated, he bears not the markings, or rather the obvious traits, of one from Olam."

A: "Though not obvious, he holds within him the twisted, linked chain of nucleides essential for immortality."

B: "If you mean the literal, physical greatly extended life actual in our genome, you must not omit the elixirs required on a regular basis to ensure such endurance, but in positive health free of disease and ailments of organ wear and tear."

A: "Yes, without those essential concoctions, from Ninhursag's laboratory and refined on Olam and only Olam, he has no hope of surviving more than six or eight hundred of their wretched years."

B: "He has five hundred years logged on Eridu [Earth] as the anthropologist for which he was trained most recently. Sustained by the elixirs brought from Olam, he performed well."

A: "And before his assignment there, he was on Lahmu [Mars] for twelve hundred years, at the Great City, helping the Second Mistress administer the various operations and functions of the Pyramid."

B: "A great honor in which he distinguished himself and received recognition from the Council of Twelve. Even king Anu commented on his outstanding performance of valuable contribution to helping base Lahmu survive."

From: Steve Canada

RE: screenwriter looking for representation

Dear Manager,

I am a writer working on a feature length screenplay that I believe your agency may be interested in representing. Please find a short pitch below for your review.

Title: "**Avenging Angels Return to Earth at End of Days**"

Genre: current day thriller

Log Line: How to stop angels from returning to Earth? How to avoid End of Days, the years of which are found Torah-encoded as between 2016 and 2020? The Pentagon tries, does its best in southern Iraq.

Pitch: All angels of all religions are found Torah-encoded, as returning at End of Days, the corrected Gregorian Calendar years of which are between 2016 and 2020. [My published book shows this].

Description: The Pentagon, working with an independent scholar [modeled after the author], tries hard but is politically dissuaded from accomplishing its mission in south-ern Iraq, where the advance return is detected to occur, of securing ancient sites used by ancient astronauts, the Anunnaki, thousands of years ago, sites they built and held sacred to their mission, in an effort to stop them from returning to Earth. Battles on-scene turn them back, with the help of Iranian nukes. The mullahs in Tehran are wait-ing for the return of their *Mahdi* and don't want any angels interfering. The *Mahdi* is also found Torah-encoded to return to that same area, also at the End of Days [as shown in my published book].

If this has piqued your interest, I could send you a hardcopy of the screenplay's Synopsis, Outline, and/or a short Treatment for your consideration. I can be contacted via email, phone or post at your earliest convenience.

Thanks, Steve Canada

From: Steve Canada

RE: screenwriter looking for representation

Dear Manager,

I am a writer working on a feature length screenplay that I believe your agency may be interested in representing. Please find a short pitch below for your review.

<u>Title</u>: THE BIBLE CODE MURDERS

<u>Genre</u>: thriller

<u>Log Line</u>: The trail of repression and murder of Torah Code researchers, rabbis cent-uries ago, continues today among independent scholars who won't be quiet or shut up and go away.

<u>Pitch</u>: Some secrets should not be revealed, especially one that shows the whole history of humanity is buried encoded in the original Hebrew text of the Torah, in its 304,805 Hebrew letters. No good can come to a person who releases it to the world.

<u>Description</u>: The trail of repression and murder of Torah Code researchers, rabbis long ago, continues today, with current scholars in the research field having to hide from threats and assassination attempts. The struggle to get legitimate recognition and even acceptance of these esoteric findings has been controversial and career-destroying for many. Broadening the application to a wide array of subjects and topics proves helpful in gaining legitimacy and credibility, and even some acceptance among skeptics. But some radical resisters still over-react, with violence as their only weapon against what they fear and don't understand. As the main character's research broadens to include all areas of human activity, in all of the past and even the future, he stirs up angry protests as his work seems to negate human free will and the popular framework of religion itself. Certain interests are fearful of what he will uncover. He barely escapes with his life before cooler heads prevail and he's accepted into a rational movement hoping to transform society in a more humane and peaceful direction.

If this has piqued your interest, I could send you a hardcopy of the screenplay's Synopsis, Outline, and/or short Treatment for your consideration. I can be contacted via email (once a week I use the public library terminals), phone (usually screened by answer machine), or post.

Thanks, Steve Canada

SASE enclosed for return of pages if no interest. Can you see this as a made-for-tv movie? Other than these 3 queries, I am working on 25 other film ideas, all in various stages of script development. Would you like to see other queries of mine?

More **Bible Code** Findings – 26 Working Film Titles:

All examples of the types of events listed below are found encoded in the Five Books of Moses (the Torah), along with names of anyone who died due to the events (see my books listed on Amazon, or at AuthorHouse.com, and Books-in-Print). A film script is developed around each event type – the story of what happens to the researcher who announces his discovery of finding such events Torah-encoded, one script per category of event – the messenger is attacked and vilified and he must fight to escape persecution, and also prove the credibility of his findings to an incredulous and frightened public.

26 working titles:

Assassination Code (4000 years of such history found encoded, starting in Egypt), Auschwitz Deaths Found Torah-Encoded [all their names], Avenging Angels of All Religions Returning to Earth at End of Days [all their names], Beheadings Code (includes French Revolution, and current 'ISIS' terror),

Car Crash Code,

Earthquake Code,

Floods Foretold,

Genocide Code,

Hiroshima Bombing Code,

Hollywood Stars' Deaths Foretold in Sacred Text (includes diseases, accidents, over- doses, suicides),

Hurricane Code,

Landslide Code,

Mass Murder Death Code,

Nagasaki Bombing Code,

Nuclear Power Plant Meltdown Code,

Plane Crashes – Airline Deaths Pre-Ordained,

Predicting U.S. Presidents [see my website www.PredictingPresidents.com],

School Shootings' Code,

Ships Sinking Code,

Terror Attacks Code,

Titanic's Destined Deaths,

Tornado Terror,

Train Wreck Code,

Tsunami Code,

Volcano Code,

War Casualties Code.

Select what Synopsis or Outlines you'd like to see, then if you like those I could send you a Treatment. If you like those, we could then discuss sending the partial or full script(s). There is obviously a potential franchise of a hero here along the lines of Indiana Jones or another scholar-adventurer confronting vested interests who would rather not have the public be aware of such a dark secret buried in a major sacred text. You might see this also as a made-for-tv series.

Thanks, Steve Canada

From: Steve Canada

RE: screenwriter looking for representation

Dear Manager,

I am a writer working on a feature length screenplay that I believe your agency may be interested in representing. Please find a short pitch below for your review.

Title: DARK MOON DEFENSE

Genre: space drama

Log Line: Secret NASA moon base on the far-side uses lasers to repel return to Earth of ancient astronauts from tenth planet of the solar system.

Pitch: A Star Wars type secret defense on the moon's dark side seems a good option to stop returning ancient astronauts who have warned of their armed return in their crop circle designs [see my 30 books that decipher crop circle designs].

Description: Far-side of the moon has been fortified in a secret Pentagon-NASA pro-gram, installing huge, powerful lasers, manned by rotations of astronauts. Official re-turn-to-the-moon to construct a permanent base on the near-side provides cover for secret laser defense program, to stop Anunnaki from returning from Nibiru to Earth.

Decades of crop circle warnings and threats given by the circle-makers, the Anun-naki of Nibiru (called 'Olam' in the bible, and 'Planet X' in popular literature) cause enough concern to Washington that the NSA, NASA and the Pentagon are tasked by the National Security Council of the White House to devise a defense plan against the returning ancient astronauts from Nibiru, tenth planet of the solar system [per ancient records and Z. Sitchin in his book series *Earth Chronicles*].

Washington is convinced the Anunnaki must be stopped from returning to Earth for another 'cultural upgrade,' because this time it could be to wipe us out. The only true rationale for invading Iraq (other than getting the WMDs there, as documented by Iraqi general Sada in his book *Saddam's Secrets*), was to occupy southern Iraq (loca-tion of ancient Sumeria, where the

Anunnaki began the first human civilization over 5000 years ago) and destroy possible Anunnaki landing sites. And deny the *Mahdi's* (the 12ᵗʰ Imam) return to Iraq (found encoded in the Torah).

If this has piqued your interest, I could send you a hardcopy of the screenplay's Synopsis, Outline, and/or short Treatment for your consideration. I can be contacted via email, phone or post at your earliest convenience.

Thanks, Steve Canada

SASE enclosed for return of pages if no interest. Would you like to see other queries of mine? Other than these 3 queries, I'm working on 25 other film ideas, all in various stages of script development, in a variety of genres (although none comedy).

From: Steve Canada

RE: screenwriter looking for representation

Dear Manager,

I am a writer working on a feature length screenplay that I believe your agency may be interested in representing. Please find a short pitch below for your review.

<u>Title</u>: DEFEATING DROUGHT – MOVING WATER

<u>Genre</u>: drama

<u>Log Line</u>: Proposed solutions to California's "water shortage" meet resistance at all political levels, backed by chambers of commerce.

<u>Pitch</u>: How can the California water policies of Democrats in Sacramento be reversed, thus saving the state from social and economic disaster?

<u>Description</u>: In certain regions of California, such as the Central Valley, part of "the fruit and veggie basket of the world," water shortages are politically motivated and imposed. Some towns there have run out of water completely, while billions of gall-ons of fresh water daily bypass them on the way to the Pacific Ocean. Denied water because the Federal EPA insisted an endangered fish be protected.

The Democrats in the legislature have intentionally designed it this way, for the purposes of increasing their stranglehold on the desperate, compliant populace, an electorate made dependent on handouts. A power base made of supplicants begging Democrats to help them.

An independently wealthy entrepreneur decides to take on the Dems in Sac'to and force them, even through shame if necessary, to reverse their restrictive water policies of not building new storage and distribution systems. And not fighting the EPA by devising a way to safely relocate the endangered "snail darter" fish of the Delta. His public relations campaign starts to make a dent in that political wall after he proposes building canals to move Midwest and Southern flood waters westward, and also dredge the Rio Grande and use freighters for water transport to the Southwest.

If this has piqued your curiosity, I could send you a hardcopy of the screenplay's Synopsis, Outline, and/or short Treatment for your consideration. I can be contacted via email, phone or post at your earliest convenience.

Thanks, Steve Canada

SASE enclosed for return of these pages if no interest.Other than these 3 queries, I'm working on over 25 other film ideas, all in various stages of script development. Might you want to see other queries of mine? Can you see this as a made for tv movie?

From: Steve Canada

RE: screenwriter looking for representation

Dear Manager,

I am a writer working on a feature length screenplay that I believe your agency may be interested in representing. Please find a short pitch below for your review.

<u>Title</u>: DEFEATING HURRICANES

<u>Genre</u>: drama-adventure

<u>Log Line</u>: weapons-grade, long-range lasers are used by the U.S. Coast Guard on ships and planes todisrupt nascent hurricanes, reducing their force to only large storms, thus saving lives and property.

<u>Pitch</u>: Coordinated efforts using the right technology can help us defeat and control gigantic storms.

<u>Description</u>: Coast Guard ship-mounted and airplane-mounted weapons-grade long range, powerful lasers are tested to disperse accumulating storms at sea that are for-ming into hurricanes, resulting in saved lives and greatly reduced property and infra-structure damage along the coast and inland.

In-fighting among and between agencies and services expose rivalries. Resistance to the program exposes the political influence behind the building industry, labor unions, insurance companies, law firms, and lending banks. Follow the money and we see why trying to defeat hurricanes this effective way hasn't been tried sooner.

Our hero, the lone voice in NOAA who conceived of and pushed for this testing program, is harassed and vilified to the point of personal bankruptcy and broken mar-riage. The media is bought-off of presenting any favorable coverage of his lone efforts to push the only successful technology that can defeat these monster storms and save lives. Proving once again that life is cheap, and rebuilding damage is green as in profitable … on a repeating basis. Business is good — mess with that at your peril.

If this has piqued your interest, I could send you a hardcopy of the screenplay's Synopsis, Outline, and/or short Treatment for your consideration. I can be contacted via email, phone or post at your earliest convenience.

Thanks, Steve Canada

SASE enclosed for return of these pages if no interest. Other than these 3 queries, I'm working on 25 other film ideas, all in various stages of script development, in a variety of genres. Might you want to see other queries of mine?

From: Steve Canada   May 9, 2016

RE: screenwriter looking for representation

Dear Manager,

I am a writer working on a feature length screenplay that I believe your agency may be interested in representing. Please find a short pitch below for your review.

Title: DOME HOUSES

Genre: drama / thriller

Log Line: Comparative structural tests show geodesic dome houses are much safer in hurricanes and tornadoes than traditional box-stick houses, an outcome threatening to architects, designers, builders, bankers, real estate developers, and insurers. Our hero architect pays the price personally and financially, as does his family, until enough po-litical and media pressure are brought to bear to save the day in the nick of time, saving lives in the next hurricane and tornado season.

Pitch: "Strangers When We Meet" meets "Atlas Shrugged."

Description: Rogue architect appeals to save lives through safer home construction, using geodesic domes as the design foundation, developed by Buckminster Fuller. He meets resistance and rejection on all fronts, especially from the construction industry, property developers, real estate agents, bankers, and insurers. Two model homes (built with his own, borrowed money) demonstrate advantages in safety and energy savings, creating some favorable media coverage and positive industry reviews.

Commercial construction approvals are denied through political pressure by estab-lished interests, creating enough tension for public concern and outcry that reverses restrictive ordinances, so more building is temporarily allowed. Public safety finally wins out over business interests that want the status quo to continue and the profits inherent in rebuilding from the total destruction of severe storms.

Such vindication saves his marriage; they reconcile and their two children learn to respect and admire him, learning life lessons in the process about courage and perseverance and integrity.

If this has piqued your interest, I could send you a hardcopy of the screenplay's Synopsis, Outline, and/or short Treatment for your consideration. I can be contacted via email, phone or post at your earliest convenience.

Thanks, Steve Canada
SASE enclosed for return of pages if no interest.

From: Steve Canada [see my 30 books, on Amazon, Books-in-Print, Author House, etc.; Google my name, as author, to see titles].

RE: screenwriter looking for representation

Dear Manager,

I am a writer working on a full length screenplay that I believe your agency may be interested in representing. Please find a short pitch below for your review.

Title: HELMET

Genre: suspense

Log Line: High school football coach designs a better, safer football helmet but is sabotaged from getting it adopted for major pro teams and schools.

Pitch: Since modern football helmets offer no better head or brain protection than those used in 1909 [fact: according to official 2016 safety testing report and media coverage], a hero needs to step up and fight the system so kids and pros alike are more protected. Can he succeed against all odds? What price safety? And at what personal sacrifice?

Description: Football helmet safety and degrees of actual protection from brain injury are hot topics in corporate boardrooms, locker rooms, league headquarters, and on campuses across the country, much less a news item now and then. Design change proposals are presented and tested, and rejected by team and school equipment buyers when price increases threaten the bottom line and profit margin of the sports program, no matter the added safety margin claims of the various designers and manufacturers(which might be based on spurious testing protocols and fudged results).

A high school football coach (whose daughter is a cheerleader and her boyfriend on the varsity team) develops a prototype in his garage workshop and has it tested. Improved protection and safety margins impress the state's athletic league, which approves it for limited use in only one county. Production financing problems pushes him to China, where the manufacturing process is undermined by graft, and the helmet does not pass testing in the U.S.

The coach is joined by the assistant coach and the school's principal in financing U.S.-based production of a limited number of helmets, for the local school district, after he convinces the school board to allow its use, to at least protect <u>their</u> children.

If this has piqued your interest, I could send you a hardcopy of the screenplay's Synopsis, Outline, and/or short Treatment for your consideration. Then, if you like those, we could discuss sending the script.

Thanks, Steve Canada
SASE enclosed for return of these pages if no interest.Other than these 3 queries, I'm working on about 36 other film ideas, all in various stages of script development. Might you want to see other queries of mine? Can you see this as a made for tv movie?

<u>From</u>: Steve Canada   May 9, 2016

<u>RE</u>: screenwriter looking for representation

Dear Manager,

I am a writer working on a feature length screenplay that I believe your agency may be interested in representing. Please find a short pitch below for your review.

<u>Title</u>: HOLLYWOOD DEATHS FORETOLD

<u>Genre</u>: drama, mystery, thriller

<u>Log Line</u>: Bible (Torah) Code reveals names of Hollywood stars and other famous people encoded, and how and when they died.

<u>Pitch</u>: Researcher gets into a lot of trouble when he resists Hollywood agents' request to apply his computer program to their clients' futures. He's in for a world of hurt after he turns down their money to apply the search program and look for specifics.

Looking at the past through the Torah's encoded truth can prove dangerous if you ask the wrong questions about the future, and deadly if the wrong people want the answers. Philip Marlowe meets Professor Langdon; 'The Long Goodbye' meets 'The Da Vinci Code.'

Description: When a desert loner scholar self-publishes 3 e-books showing how the Bible (Torah) Code reveals how and when Hollywood stars and other rich and famous people died, of what specific disease or accident, or suicide, or by overdose [see these 3 books for sale on Amazon, and see enclosed article on author regarding interview for the History Channel], his life gets complicated when he's contacted by living stars' agents who want to know the predictive power of the Code, and dangerous when he hesitates to run the computer program searches or interpret them or verify them, for any price. They don't understand his reluctance, and take certain measures to change his mind. What transpires is a battle of wills, one that everyone loses. Death rears its ugly head, and people learn lessons no one was meant to learn. Found encoded in the past is an unexpected future only a sacred text could reveal.

If this has piqued your interest, I could send you a hardcopy of the screenplay's Synopsis, Outline, and/or short Treatment for your consideration. I can be contacted via email, phone or post at your earliest convenience.

Thanks, Steve Canada
SASE enclosed for return of pages if no interest.

From: Steve Canada   May 9, 2016

RE: screenwriter looking for representation

Dear Manager,

I am a writer working on a feature length screenplay that I believe your agency may be interested in representing. Please find a short pitch below for your review.

Title: ICEBERG SOLUTION – DROUGHT BUSTER

Genre: drama / thriller

Log Line: Proposal by a sea-going engineering firm to tow two icebergs to the California coast, one from off Alaska to the Central Coast, and one from Antarctica to the Southern Coast, as a long-term solution to the severe drought devastating the economy of the state and the southwest brings on political conflict and business rivalries that threaten established and environmental interests.

Pitch: Political clashes and greed thwart viable solution to long-term drought in California and in parts of the northwest and the southwest. Current interest story exposes conflicts inherent in potential workable solution to growing, extreme water shortage.

Description: Desperation for a dependable fresh water supply drives the populace to vote for a referendum to accomplish the engineering firm's proposal. Both parts of the project are deemed too complicated and expensive if the huge icebergs are parked off-shore and melt-water siphoned off into ships which bring the water to shore, off-loading at pumping stations for pipeline transport inland and to local and coastal towns, cities, farms and orchards.

The alternative is to bring the icebergs to the shore close enough for flexible piping to collect the melt-runoff, but not too close to cause unacceptable environmental damage to the coast's ecology. The politics around each phase and each part of the project are harsh, dirty and deadly.

If this has piqued your interest, I could send you a hardcopy of the screenplay's Synopsis, Outline, and/or short Treatment for your consideration. I can be contacted via email, phone or post at your earliest convenience.

Thanks, Steve Canada

From: Steve Canada

RE: screenwriter looking for representation

Dear Manager,

I am a writer working on a feature length screenplay that I believe your agency may be interested in representing. Please find a short premise, logline, and description below for your review.

<u>Title</u>: JIHAD COMFORT

<u>Genre</u>: terrorism thriller

<u>Premise</u>: Fact: comfort animals are allowed on airplanes with passengers, in passenger seats (see recent CNN investigative report). Fact: certificate authorizing comfort animals are available online for free and without any medical consultation or verification. This can be exploited by terrorists to carry, unchallenged and unscreened, bomb-ladened simulated animals onboard airplanes, trains, subways, ships, buses, and into restaurants, concerts, arenas, and into any government building or crowded mall.

<u>Log Line</u>: ISIS terror operatives in U.S. arrange for 100 suicide bombers to use 100 simulated comfort animals (in this case, pot-bellied pigs, as was used in the CNN re-port of late March 2016) to blow up 25 airliners in coordinated attacks, along with simultaneous attacks at 25 malls, 25 government buildings, and 25 trains, subways and buses, spread all over the country.

<u>Description</u>: A terror operation exploiting yet another gap in American security, the loophole of comfort animals allowed on all forms of public transportation in the U.S. All that's needed for "permission" is a faux certificate authorizing such accompaniment, a free online certificate that is received without any medical screening or conversation with anyone. The plot is successful

and thousands of innocent civilians and government workers are killed, ushering in a new day in America, of marshal law and Draconian security measures.

First plan was an operation of 1000 comfort animals; suicide bombers hitting 1000 targets, but its unwieldy scale was deemed unfeasible, so a smaller target list was fin-ally agreed upon. Operatives were recruited, including some ISIS members who recently crossed the southern border with illegal migrants from Central America and Mexico, and some rained in remote camps in the U.S., exclusive Muslim enclaves where Sharia law is practiced and enforced.; others trained in cities or small towns.

If this has piqued your interest, I could send you a hardcopy of the screenplay's Synopsis, Outline, and/or short Treatment for your consideration. I can be contacted via email, phone or post at your earliest convenience. You wonder if this could make a decent tv feature, or even a "24" episode.

Thanks, Steve Canada

From: Steve Canada

RE: screenwriter looking for representation

Dear Manager,

I am a writer working on a feature length screenplay that I believe your agency may be interested in representing. Please find a short description below for your review.

Title: KILLING TORNADOES

Genre: thriller, adventure

Log Line: in a quest to save lives and avoid destruction of property and livelihoods, a private inventor develops a van-mounted powerful laser designed to disperse the moisture and wind of a tornado's funnel, greatly reducing the storm's destructive force and power. "Slice and dice that twister!"

Pitch: "Tornado Road" meets "Storm Riders" meets "Tornado Alley" meets "Storm Chasers."

Description: Loner inventor, whose parents were killed by a tornado (they died in the home he grew up in), is frustrated at every turn in trying to demonstrate his powerful, long-range laser to government agencies that should be interested in such a weapon against destructive tornadoes in "Tornado Alley," the group of U.S. States most affected every year where dozens are killed and billions of dollars of damage is done.

He strikes out on his own to prove that it works, and saves lives and property in several towns. Hailed as a hero by some, he is vilified as a dangerous prank by the housing industry, insurers, real estate developers, and bankers, and threatened with legal action by the EPA and State Safety Boards.

People and churches rally around him and his cause, and expose the authorities as frauds who do not actually have the public's safety as their first priority. Well that is about to change if entrenched and powerful moneyed interests can be dislodged from their comfortable political club.

If this has piqued your interest, I could send you a hardcopy of the screenplay's Synopsis, Outline and/or short Treatment for your consideration. I can be contacted via email, phone or post at your earliest convenience. You wonder if this could also make a decent tv feature.

Thanks, Steve Canada

From: Steve Canada

RE: screenwriter looking for representation

Dear Manager,

I am a writer working on a feature length screenplay that I believe your agency may be interested in representing. Please find a short pitch below for your review.

Title: PEACE (CHEM) TRAILS

Genre: drama-mystery

Log Line: Chemical analysis of "chem trails" by independent lab shows residual molecules used in brain research to decrease nerve network activity of the brain's "belief center."

Pitch: Wars and hatred are universally religion-based, which in turn rely on certain nerve pathways in the brain. Interrupt and decrease that brain activity for less hatred and fewer and smaller wars, resulting in greater peace in the world.

Description: U.S. Government test program of aerial spraying specific chemicals at altitude that target certain brain nerve networks associated with religious belief has policy implications beyond war and peace. It goes to chemical mind control and population reduction.

Love triangle at lab twists motivation that undermines credibility of attempt to ex-pose this secret government program aimed at altering people, society and history.

War is big business and profit-driven, employing millions of willing participants. The forces against peace are profoundly powerful. Influential through the standard channels of industrial, financial and political centers of power, our independent investigators uncover a hidden rationale for the "Chem Trail" program … attitude control, easier brainwashing, and decrease in libido, along with unexpected side-effect – lower sperm count worldwide, implying population control and eventual reduction of current seven billion people, which far exceeds the carrying capacity of the planet.

Who is telling the U.S. Government to do this, and how many other countries are cooperating?

If this has piqued your curiosity, I could send you a hardcopy of the screenplay's Synopsis, Outline, and/or short Treatment for your consideration. I can be contacted via email, phone or post at your earliest convenience.

Thanks, Steve Canada

SASE enclosed for return of these pages if no interest.Other than these 3 queries, I'm working on over 25 other film ideas, all in various stages of script development. Might you want to see other queries of mine? Can you see this as a made for tv movie?

From: Steve Canada

RE: screenwriter looking for representation

Dear Manager,

I am a writer working on a feature length screenplay that I believe your agency may be interested in representing. Please find a short pitch below for your review.

Title: PLANE CRASHES BIBLE -CODE PREDICTED – AIRLINE DEATHS FORE-TOLD

Genre: mystery / thriller

Log Line: Plane crashes and names of airline crash victims are found Torah-encoded, between Genesis 42-11 and Deuteronomy 13:19, along with the airline name, make and model of the airplane, and crash location and date.

[Published sample book page of mine available upon request, showing encoded:

"TWA flight 800, Rome, Italy, Boeing 707, November, 1964, plane crash"]. Revealing this research finding sets off a chain reaction of deadly threats to the discoverer, endangering him and his family.

Pitch: "Why Planes Crash" meets secret bible code. The Torah's sacred text truth is taken as a threat to the airline industry and by government officials overseeing flight safety and public relations of perceived threats to airline security. The potential wide-spread economic impact is profound.

Description: Allowing this information out would greatly damage the U.S. economy, and the world's, so dependent as it is on air travel and transport. Attempts to suppress this discovery of a desert-dwelling scholar loner proves deadly as he tries to protect himself and his family from forces he never imagined protecting the corporate, banking, investment, and insurance industry interests behind selling safety to the traveling public. He barely escapes with his life.

If this has piqued your interest, I could send you a hardcopy of the screenplay's Synopsis, Outline, and/or a short Treatment for your consideration. I can be contacted via email, phone or post at your earliest convenience.

Thanks, Steve Canada

From: Steve Canada [see my 30 books, on Amazon, Books-in-Print, Author House, etc.; Google my name, as author, to see titles].

RE: screenwriter looking for representation

Dear Manager,

I am a writer working on a full length screenplay that I believe your agency may be interested in representing. Please find a short pitch below for your review.

Title: SECEDE!

Genre: political thriller

Log Line: In the not too distant future the southwestern U.S. states vote to secede, and join Mexico in political union. California breaks into North and South, and the South joins in seceding.

Pitch: Growing rebellion among Hispanic population in U.S. leads to popular uprising, and separatist movement as their population proportion grows to over 50 percent in the border states.

Description: Economic depression and growing factionalism are seen by the radical group La Raza as opportunity to reestablish "Azatlan," ancient land of pre-Mexico. Breakdown of civil order precipitates popular movement to realign allegiances officially and join in legal union with Mexico. All social factions of educators, lawyers, bankers, legislators, etc., contribute to the breakaway.

Threats of invasion, occupation and martial law by the other states are quelled by Congress. Economic conditions are so bad, advantages of doing without such a rebellious population are put in stark relief when disadvantages of forcing the union to stay together are objectively analyzed. Families and neighborhoods are torn apart. Dissenters try to legally reverse the separatist decision and are attacked by mobs waving Mexican flags and burning American flags.

Final resolution is a redefining of borders, identity and allegiances. Situational identity is clarified with social psychology of identity politics. Adaptation to new circumstances lends positive attitude.

If this has piqued your interest, I could send you a hardcopy of the screenplay's Synopsis, Outline, and/or short Treatment for your consideration. Then, if you like those, we could discuss sending the script.

Thanks, Steve Canada
SASE enclosed for return of these pages if no interest. Other than these 3 queries, I'm working on about 36 other film ideas, all in various stages of script development. Might you want to see more of my queries? Can you see this as a made for tv movie?

From: Steve Canada

RE: screenwriter looking for representation

Dear Manager,

I am a writer working on a feature length screenplay that I believe your agency may be interested in representing. Please find a short pitch below for your review.

<u>Title</u>: SECRET MISSION TO OLAM

<u>Genre</u>: alien contact thriller

<u>Log Line</u>: Secret Pentagon-NASA manned spacecraft mission to tenth planet of the solar system, Nibiru, called 'Olam' in the bible and 'Planet X' in popular culture, home-world of the Anunnaki, ancient astronauts who created humans and began every major civilization on Earth, starting with Sumeria about 5000 years ago, located in southern Iraq. NASA astronauts negotiate for humanity's survival.

<u>Pitch</u>: Can astronauts as diplomats convince our progenitor "aliens" not to destroy humanity? What leverage do they have to negotiate with, or are they just powerless supplicants begging to be spared? What can they offer? What do they have to bargain with? Have they been given enough authority and 'chips' to bargain with effectively? Do the Olamians actually <u>need</u> something from humans only they can give? What allowance for failure has been figured into the trip's planning, what fall-back position?

<u>Description</u>: Decades of England's crop circle warnings contained in their designs and ancient symbols are taken seriously by the U.S. Space Command and NASA. They enlist the help of the White House's National Security Council, who in turn reaches out to a secret Pentagon group

for planning and logistics of a manned mission to Nibiru. Three astronauts are selected and trained, with a back-up crew on stand-by. Plan is to open negotiations and hopefully convince the Olamians (the Anunnaki, ancient astronauts who genetically engineered humans) not to destroy humanity, to ask what people need to do to change in ways that would warrant continued survival. The Olamian demands are stark and harsh, but the only choice if humanity is to be allowed to survive.

If this has piqued your interest, I could send you a hardcopy of the screenplay's Synopsis, Outline, and/or a short Treatment for your consideration. I can be contacted via email (once a week I use the public library terminals), phone (usually screen through answer machine), or post.

Thanks, Steve Canada

Wim Wenders the German director told me face to face some years ago, after I gave him one of my 30 books on decoding and interpreting crop circle designs, that he "might some day make a crop circle movie." My script at this point is only at the outline stage but will get more attention after I work up queries on some of my 25 other film ideas, which are at various stages of script development.

See my books on crop circles at Books-in-Print, and on Amazon, among other places.

If you come across some of these titles for sale at between $200 and $300, these are from collectors who long ago bought copies directly from me (as self-publisher, the only source) and waited til the rare-books market grew enough. They are mistaken though, because they did not go out of print, copies of them are sitting on my shelves, and the masters from which I photocopied them and had them bound at the local copy shop.

From: Steve Canada

RE: screenwriter looking for representation

Dear Manager,

I am a writer working on a feature length screenplay that I believe your agency may be interested in representing. Please find a short pitch below for your review.

Working Title: TERROR ATTACK DEATHS FORETOLD IN SACRED TEXT

Genre: mystery / thriller

Log Line: All terror attacks and names of victims are found Torah-encoded, between Exodus 39:29 and Leviticus 13:25, with a skip of 1019 letters to find the Key word encoded, with a less than one in a million chance of finding it encoded in the whole Torah. [See my 2015 book *Event Code Uncovered*, Figures 24-26; and my 2013 book *Death's Bible Code*, pages 45 to54; and enclosed newspaper article about my inter-view for the History Channel].

<u>Premise</u>: whoever discovers such a secret and publishes it is in for a world of hurt.

<u>Description</u>: Andre Adanac, 58, a desert-dwelling loner scholar, releases his research discoveries of secrets encoded in the Torah, the Five Books of Moses. One of the many areas of inquiry he has explored is terror attacks worldwide, finding all their specifics, including names of victims, clearly encoded. Publishing these astounding results be-comes controversial and personally troubling, and puts him in danger from authorities who suspect he knows more than he lets on and want to know if he can use his computer program to predict the future, and terror groups who fear the same thing. As a tar-get, his life and marriage are in shambles as he struggles to save his sanity and keep his wits about him so he can continue his work and protect his family. All he wants is to be left alone in peace.

If this has piqued your interest, I could send you a hardcopy of the screenplay's Synopsis, Outline, and/or short Treatment for your consideration. I can be contacted via email (once a week I use the public library terminals), phone (usually screened through answer machine), or post.

Thanks, Steve Canada

From: Steve Canada

RE: screenwriter looking for representation

Dear Manager,

I am a writer working on a feature length screenplay that I believe your agency may be interested in representing. Please find a short pitch below for your review.

<u>Title</u>: TITANIC'S DESTINED DEATHS

<u>Genre</u>: mystery, drama

<u>Log Line</u>: Valiant effort to reverse Titanic's fate, discovered secretly encoded in the Books of Moses, has the ring of historical truth to it we can only admire.

<u>Pitch</u>: A remake of "Titanic" but with the drama of injecting a character who has dis-covered the ship's fate and who does his best to save it and cheat destiny.

<u>Description</u>: An Oxford University professor, whose sideline is Bible Code research, in 1911 discovers encoded in the Books of Moses the fate of the Titanic (which sank on April 15, 1912), then under construction in Ireland, and tries to warn the company's executives, unsuccessfully. He and his beautiful grad student assistant on board ship can't convince the captain to change course. They almost die during the sinking.

Names of all victim's of Titanic's sinking are found encoded in the Torah, between Genesis 40:17 and Leviticus 21:5 [see my 2013 book *Death's Bible Code*].

Intrigue develops when nautical historians research other ships that have sunk and the names of the passengers and crew who perished, verifying they're all found Torah-encoded. Bankers and insurers get concerned once word gets out, causing potential market and business decline as authorities attempt to put a lid on a growing news story. The discoverer of this connection must be stopped. Too much is at stake for the truth to be fully revealed to a trusting traveling public.

If this has piqued your interest, I could send you a hardcopy of the screenplay's Synopsis, Outline, and/or short Treatment for your consideration. I can be contacted via email, phone or post at your earliest convenience.

Thanks, Steve Canada

From: Steve Canada

RE: screenwriter looking for representation

Dear Manager,

I am a writer working on a feature length screenplay that I believe your agency may be interested in representing. Please find a short pitch below for your review.

Title: VOLCANO CODE

Genre: adventure-mystery

Log Line: history of deadly volcano eruptions are found encoded in the Torah, the Five Books of Moses, by eccentric Bible Code researcher Stef Kanata – his warning local authorities saves lives.

Pitch: Dedicated to saving lives and property using his Bible Code searches for deadly volcanoes proves worth his time and effort once he is able to convince authorities to heed the warnings.

Description: If past is prologue, then tracing down names of those killed in past deadly volcano eruptions and finding them encoded in the Torah, between Genesis 1:1 and Exodus 36:33, could help verify valid application of the Code to future eruptions. Stef Kanat's predictive model proves all too real for a Hawaii volcano and nearby residents as they flee for their lives.

Cultural anthropologist Dart Velcrom and ethnologist Ann DeCosta at Colorado State University in Denver clue him to the complexity of name tracing in pre-literate tribal societies when he asks for their help with identifying some of the victims of the Krakatoa volcano eruption in the Dutch East Indies in 1883, when at least 36,417 people were killed by the generated massive tsunami.

The location and year are found Torah-encoded. Dart and Ann are suitably impressed, and are willing to help him any way they can. They take time off and accompany him on his expeditions as he tries to save lives and prevent property destruction by warning local inhabitants. Trouble is, local authorities don't appreciate these foreigners coming in and upsetting the populace and disturbing the economy of the tourist trade, no matter how convincing Stef's code-based predictions are.

If this has piqued your curiosity, I could send you a hardcopy of the screenplay's Synopsis, Outline, and/or short Treatment for your consideration. I can be contacted via email, phone or post at your earliest convenience.

Thanks, Steve Canada
SASE enclosed for return of these pages if no interest.Other than these 3 queries, I'm working on over 25 other film ideas, all in various stages of script development. Might you want to see other queries of mine? Can you see this as a made for tv movie?

PART 3: 19 MORE FILM IDEAS; PROPOSALS AND TREATMENTS:

see descriptions, below the list, in numerical order -- ('Code'
refers to topic found encoded in the Torah).

1   Assassination Code
2   Beheadings Code
3   Car Crash Code
4   Earthquake Code
5   Fireproof Houses
6   Genocide Code
7   Holy Flood!
8   Holy Landslide!
9   Lower The Seas, Save the Planet
10 The Museum Immortal
11 Nuke Plant Meltdown Code
12 Predicting U.S. Presidents
13 Saving Russia (or 'To Save Russia')
14 School and Mass Shootings Code
15 Store the Heat, Save the Planet
16 Train Crash Code
17 Tsunami Code
18 War Deaths' Code
19 WW II A-Bombs Code

Three more short movie proposals are added after those above:
"Dirty Bomb School Buses," "Election Repair," and "Legal Ivory"

1. Title: **Assassination Code** – All Assassinations Throughout History Found
1 Torah-Encoded. From 4000 years ago to today – who, where, when – names, places, dates. (See
my 2010 book *Foretold in Sacred Code,* Part 4, pp. 91-119; and also see my 2013 book *Death's Bible
Code,* pages 5-12 for examples and Torah Matrices).

Genre: political intrigue

LogLine: scholar becomes a target when he reveals he has discovered all assassinations encoded in
the Five Books of Moses, in the original Hebrew.

Pitch: Independent, loner researcher unexpectedly exposes himself to threats when he publishes
his findings in the encoded Torah that show all assassinations throughout history, even that of an
Egyptian Pharaoh 4000 years ago (before the Torah was written) is clearly encoded in the sacred text.

Description: Scholarly loner naively thinks his astounding discovery will have no repercussions in the political world, where threat of assassination is a reality every government must deal with and protect against, at great cost and use of manpower.

Key players can't understand why, since he has found all of the past encoded in the Five Books of Moses, he can't also find the future buried in there also. Trying to persuade him to unlock the text to knowledge of future assassinations becomes a major effort, first using enticement, then friendly persuasion, then graduated motivation trying to convince him to cooperate in helping defend their principals.

When his search results are too vague for their taste, more direct and serious per-suasion techniques are employed, but to no avail, since it becomes clear he needs a lot more time to clarify relevant Torah search parameters for future events. At least that's what he claims. All they want to know is 'Who's Next' and if their guy is a target that will be successfully knocked off.

2. Title: **Beheadings Code**

Genre: Political Thriller

LogLine: scholar-adventurer becomes a target when he reveals his discovery of all beheadings in recorded history are found encoded in the Torah, including all names, places and dates, including the bloody French Revolution, and ISIL beheadings of American journalists and others.

Pitch: same as for the 'Assassinations' Code movie.

Description: Bible Code researcher Stef Kanat, adventurer and man about town, endangers himself and his team trying to save those he identifies as in danger, in his attempt to reverse inevitability of destiny as found Torah-encoded.

3. Title: **Car Crash Code**

Genre: Mystery

LogLine: Deadly car crashes are discovered by independent researcher to be Torah-encoded, including the car's make and model, the date, the location, and the name(s) of the victim(s).

Pitch: Can safety be improved using this researcher's method? If he'll cooperate with authorities in trying to predict deadly car crashes, thus possibly saving many lives on the deadly highways of America where tens of thousands of people die every year.

Description: Scholarly, loner Bible Code researcher discovers deadly car crashes are encoded in the Torah, including the names of those killed, the date, the location, and make and model of the vehicle(s) involved. He tries to keep his findings to himself until he can figure out the implications, and wrestles with the moral questions of possibly saving lives if people can be warned in time, if he can somehow figure out how to predict the crashes.

Word spreads among his few friends and family members, until a reporter picks up on a possible story, and contacts him to learn more about his discoveries and what it might mean, and how it could be used to help road and driving safety. The story gets out, and research funding is provided. His gorgeous assistant helps with mainframe programming and read-out interpretation. Media coverage distorts their work, and religious fanatics attack them, even though they have a body guard.

He is reluctant to take responsibility for predicting specific events, but is persuaded to at least try and predict particular crashes, after the story breaks and he is contacted by a foundation that funds transportation safety programs. Mainframe computer time is reserved for him. He and a gorgeous foundation assistant devise search techniques for multiple input parameters for search protocols using his Bible Code computer program he acquired from Israel.

Masses of data filtered through algorithms they devise for this specific purpose pinpoint likely car crashes at certain locations and times. Alerts go out to the police, and deadly accidents are apparently averted, because no accidents occur where and when indicated. Can fate be interfered with? Can destiny be changed?

But how accurate were the projections, actually? Did other deadly car accidents happen nearby around that time that were not indicated in the Torah search results? Were lives actually saved? Since there are too many variables and possible outcomes to account for any one event or non-event, all they can do is assume they did some good by possibly preventing a deadly accident at the specified place and time.

He and his assistants are viewed by the public and written about in the press as if they are seers or witches using dark magic to peer into the future where death might take victims of car accidents. Some religious zealots even accuse them of plotting with Satan to <u>cause </u>the deadly accidents, using evil modern technology to pry into the forbidden knowledge of the future, which they claim is solely God's domain to influence and control. They claim that trying to interfere with God's plan is the work of the Devil himself., and their work must be condemned and stopped because it is an affront to God and his loving will.

They are assigned an armed escort guard, but he proves inadequate when a group of flag-waving fundamentalist Christians attack them on the sidewalk, sending them to the hospital with injuries that take several days of treatment. Will they abandon their research? How determined are they in their campaign to save the lives of drivers? How much are they willing to sacrifice themselves in their mission to protect people?

4. Title: **Earthquake Code**
(see my 2013 book *Death's Bible Code,* pp.29-31 for Torah Matrix examples)

<u>Genre:</u> adventure-mystery.

Logline: researcher discovers history of deadly earthquakes encoded in the Torah.

Pitch: 'Indiana Jones' is harassed for his findings and finds fulfillment in far away places.

Description: Eccentric Bible Code researcher Stef Kanat discovers the history of deadly earthquakes as Torah-encoded, and pays the price for revealing his findings. All hell breaks loose when he agrees to try and predict a major quake. Secrets betrayed can be dangerous.

The Torah text Matrix search Key is "--------," as transliterated, and found en-coded from Genesis 35:19 to Leviticus 7:12; skip ---- letters to find the Key encoded.

5. Title: **Fireproof Houses**

Genre: thriller

Logline: trying to make houses fireproof threatens the income of too many interests.

Pitch: don't fight the profit-making power of fire if you don't want to get burned.

Description: Made available to the public for purchase would be an organic foam spray kit for sale in preparation for any fire that endangers the structure. The effort to develop, test, perfect, market, advertize and distribute this privately developed pro-duct is interfered with at every turn. Those who have an interest in seeing houses burned to the ground (such as real estate developers, construction companies, suppliers, appraisers, agents, unions) do their best to prevent the public from having easy and ready access to this life and property saving product. Is our hero fighting a losing battle? Will he and his family be able to survive the pressure, threats and harassment?

6. Title: **Genocide Code**
(see my 2013 book *Death's Bible Code*, pp.13-15, for Auschwitz, and Chelmno camps; names are found encoded and shown encoded in an unpublished manuscript).

Genre: mystery-adventure

Logline: location and calendar of genocides in history are found Torah-encoded.

Pitch: can future genocides be avoided by knowing their past-encoded history in the sacred Torah?

Description: rogue researcher Stef Kanat and his team attempt to interfere with the next location of a genocide as discovered encoded in the Torah, to try and divert fate from its appointed conjunction with murder and death. Can 'future' recorded history be undone? What price would such a violation of destiny cast upon current history and those trying to alter it or keeping it from happening?

7. <u>Title</u>: **Holy Flood!**

<u>Genre</u>: mystery-adventure

<u>Logline</u>: All floods are found clearly encoded in the Five Books of Moses (the Torah).

<u>Pitch</u>: can further flooding damage and deaths be avoided by finding floods Torah-en-coded and warning enough people?

<u>Description</u>: rogue Bible Code researcher Stef Kanat and his team attempt to interfere with the dire effects of Mother Nature, namely finding future floods encoded in the Torah, and warning authorities. After he is repeatedly ignored and written off as some sort of crackpot nut and people die and much property damage occurs, an intrepid investigative reporter takes a keen interest in his work and starts to write about his discoveries and genuine efforts to save lives and avoid massive property and infrastructure damage. Finally a county board of supervisors takes heed and follows his precautions, thus avoiding much damage and destruction and loss of life in the next flash flood.

He's hailed as a hero, and goes state-wide with his program, and later national, and is considered a hero from coast to coast. He's urged to run for state office, which he resists, at least for now. The glint in his eye might mean he has in mind some national office he could run for soon.

8. <u>Title</u>: **Holy Landslide!**

<u>Genre</u>: mystery-thriller

<u>Logline</u>: Bible Code researcher discovers that all landslides and mudslides are found clearly encoded in the Five Books of Moses, the Torah.

<u>Pitch</u>: the names of those killed in deadly land and mud slides are found encoded in the Torah, so how to predict them and warn people to escape?

<u>Description</u>: death and destruction from land and mud slides can be avoided if we could only predict where and when they will strike. Our hero does just that, but in a way not easily accepted, so he tries to enlist willing partners to convince at least <u>some</u> officials to give his predictive model a chance.

After some minor setbacks and resistance (such as "interfering in God's work is evil"), a few successful predictions lead to a test operation of warning and evacuation, saving lives. More widespread adoption of his method saves even more lives, around the world. He is honored for his ground-breaking work as he keeps trying to have it used in more countries.

9. <u>Title</u>: **Lower the Seas, Save the Planet**

<u>Genre</u>: mystery-thriller-adventure

<u>Logline</u>: Obama quote: "This will be the season the seas stopped rising."

<u>Pitch</u>: If the Earth is hollow enough with large caverns, as some claim, why can't at least one hole get punched through the mantle's crust on the sea floor and act as a drain to lower the level of the rising seas (which is apparently caused by global warming, melting the ice caps)?

<u>Thesis</u>: Geological formations of empty, air-filled undersea caverns might be located in enough numbers and size to make a difference, when filled with seawater, to lower the average sea level by up to an inch. This first phase of the project would prove the technology and its effectiveness. Continuing with a further search for more large under sea caverns would require greater international cooperation and investment on a multilateral basis, in a concerted effort to lower planet-wide sea levels.

The total volume of the caverns discovered required to lower the worldwide sea level by an inch could be calculated: total surface area x one inch; convert to cubic feet or yards and you'll know the volume needed for the first inch of sea-level lower-ing. Staying ahead of the rate of sea-level rising is only part of the equation. Making up for the rise already detected in the past recent decades would require a massive international effort. To keep up with the rate of rising (1/8th of an inch a year?) will re-quire another scale of cooperation and investment.

A sea floor search for such caverns under the sea floor could locate potential storage space for a massive volume of sea water, enough to lower the seas' rising level enough to remove the encroaching threat low-lying cities and islands.

The city in greatest danger (apparently in the world, according to a recent report) is Miami, Florida. Two feet of water rise would inundate it completely. The estimated cost of defending it with barriers runs to nearly four trillion dollars, according to the same report.

<u>Description</u>: The funding and manning of such a sea water storage project, based on a plan developed by a rogue oceanographer, is the focus of the beginning of this film.

Act 1 lays out the problem and issue and threat facing countries and cities around the world, including South Sea island nations facing complete obliteration as global warming continues to melt the ice caps and causing sea level rises planet-wide. Various proposals for trying to stop the water rise are explored, as international conferences and the United Nations struggle with arriving at viable options that are cost-effective.

Act 2 introduces our hero and his controversial plan to punch through the Earth's crust at the most likely spots where geological studies have revealed a thin enough crust layer and cavities below large enough to hold enough water to make a measurable difference in lowering sea level. No one is convinced, and funding is insufficient for his team to proceed with test drilling, except a small group of billionaires who see a project with enough payoff to make a difference in their quest to make a real difference in their contribution to mankind.

Sample exchange at a planning meeting:

"The Crust Puncher deep-sea craft – here's a slide of a diagram of its configuration and layout – will locate the spots on the sea floor where the Earth's crust is thinnest. At those various locations the puncher craft will drill through the crust, having done a sonar measuring of the volume of the vacancy, or void."

"Yes, I agree. That's all well and good, but there must be a measurable limit to it, so too much of the ocean doesn't leak into the inner mantle, or even the core, creating spouts of geyser steam we can't cap or control."

"Even that could be a source of new energy for power generation if we're smart about it."

"Yes, we must prepare for that as an exploitable resource, but what I'm trying to emphasize here is the potential for draining too much of the ocean too quickly. If we can measure the approximate volume of the voids, even if they are composed of a series of interlocked fissures and caverns, we at least could estimate how much the seas would be lowered when they are filled with seas water."

"Only if we can map the extent of those voids, no matter how they're-structured. We've got a lot of careful and thorough mapping to do, so we need a special team on that, and the sooner the better. We don't have the luxury of years of study here."

Act 3 shows the organizing struggles, personality conflicts, sabotage coming from various sources, and undermining from competing and rival interests, and setbacks as they push the project forward, overcoming resistance, skepticism within the ranks, and bureaucratic inertia. Final victory comes when four different areas of likely cavern candidates are located, after several failed attempts to punch through the sea floor, and to caverns that proved too small. Control pumps with valves, as flow regulators, are installed, so the lowering of the sea level is not too fast or drastic. Hailed as heroes, and rewarded for their efforts, the team moves on to the next phase of the project, greater positive control over regulating sea levels around the world.

10. Title: **Museum Immortal**

Genre: drama-mystery

Logline: British royals share knowledge of immortal DNA found in British Museum's ancient hybrid specimen of a demi-goddess with only European royals, repressing knowledge of it for everyone else, keeping potential extreme longevity to themselves.

Pitch: the lure of immortality is stronger than all moral rules. Royalty will pay any price to live greatly extended lives in good health, and keep the secret for themselves.

Premise: factually documented archaeological findings in Z. Sitchin's 2010 book, *There Were Giants Upon the Earth – Gods, Demigods, and Human Ancestry: the Evidence of Alien DNA*, reveal

British Natural History Museum's refusal to DNA test two specific remains Sitchin claims could show alien DNA presence on Earth (see pp.343-6 of his book).

Description: Assistant British Natural History Museum director alerts the director about a letter from Z. Sitchin asking for permission to test remains of "Queen Puabi" and "Prince Meskalaindug." This piques the director's curiosity but he replies with a standard policy of not testing any specimens in the museum's possession. He's curious also about Sitchin's claim that alien DNA might be found in the tissue of these spec-mens, who Sitchin identified as an Anunnaki goddess (not a 'queen') *Nin.Puabi*, and a demigod (not a Sumerian 'prince'), *Mes.kalam.dug.*

He realizes the royal family has been interested in life extension for a long time, even to the point of following the research progress of the Life Extension Foundation in Florida, and ordering some of their unique supplements, and attending the foundation's Life Extension conferences. At the next social function where a member of the royal family is in attendance, he makes a point of mentioning the Sitchin letter about two unique specimens of remains that Sitchin claims could contain alien-hybrid DNA, which in itself could suggest extreme longevity, given the cultural history of those beings, as recorded by the Sumerians about four thousand years ago.

The family member takes the message back to Buckingham Palace and mentions it to Prince Philip, a main mover in the family on the question of life extension and good health. He calls the museum director and arranges a private visit, at which he confirms the presence of the two specimens in question and the documentation of their origins at a ruins at *Ur* (south of Baghdad), dug up in 1927. He requests confidential approval for secret testing of the remains, which the director reluctantly approves.

Prince Philip, who learned long ago that "kingship was lowered from Heaven," arranges for a small research team to visit the museum to examine the remains and take tiny tissue samples for lab examination and DNA mapping. These tests reveal an extraordinary hybrid-DNA mix, with special elements that distinguish it as unique. The demi-goddess was murdered, so her DNA matrix showed no sign of life-ending shortening of telomeres to any extreme extent.

Seeing how the royalty of Europe are related to each other through intermarriage, many marriages of which were arranged on the basis of political alliances, with an eye to mutual benefit and obligation, the shared DNA across royal lineages could easily be detected with a simple mitachondria test for a maternal line of descendants. Compatibility with the museum's specimens' DNA could be measured and protocols followed for degrees of infusion indicated as most favorable to affect longevity (the biochemistry details of which would not be divulged by the experimenters).

"With this knowledge we can bio-engineer our own evolution, or at least make a good start with extending our lifespans, while maintaining good health."

Private couriers and secret communiques relay the outline of a plan to thoroughly test all European royal family members. Confidentiality is sworn to in a binding obligation of inter-family trust. The solemn ceremonies of oath are made in private and in secret.

A pang of conscience in a young subject starts a gossip string that reaches her uncle, who is loathe to discipline her appropriately. Various pretenders to assorted thrones learn of the inner circle's plan to genetically extend their own lifespans but keep such enhancement to only their family circle.

"That's why a directive to the humans in the Garden of Eden was to stay away from the Tree of Life. DNA is the key to inheritance, which is the Tree of Life itself. So I hope we don't need to learn that lesson the hard way."

"As long as we don't allow this secret to seep out into public knowledge, we should be able to maintain our advantage indefinitely."

11. <u>Title</u>: **Nuke Plant Meltdown Code**

<u>Genre</u>: disaster-thriller

<u>Logline</u>: Torah Code researcher finds nuclear power plant meltdowns encoded in the sacred text, to his great regret when he lets the word out.

<u>Pitch</u>: revealing too much about finding nuclear power plant meltdowns secretly encoded in the sacred text of the Torah can get you branded a nut case, even if the text's truth is inescapable. No matter, there are large forces at work, such as large investors who don't like their bottom line threatened by making their financial backers uneasy when the public's fear reaches the political realm of decision makers.

<u>Description</u>: our curious scholar can't avoid trouble once he uncovers a verifiable fact encoded in the Five Books of Moses – the meltdown of various nuclear power plants around the world, such as at Chernobl in Ukraine, Three Mile Island in the U.S., and Fukushima in Japan (see the author's 2013 book *Death's Bible Code*, pp.32-34; 'Fukushima' as the Key is found encoded from Numbers 19:14 to Deuteronomy 14:21 – skip 2269 letters to find the Key encoded; all factors of the event are found encoded).

Not only are the governments involved in these countries concerned that such events are revealed in a sacred text of a major religion, but that superstitious followers worldwide might blame <u>them</u> for the evil unleashed by their ineptitude and bad decisions.

Can this troublesome monk researcher be silenced, or perhaps co-opted, or even sidelined with distractions or new directions of his funded research? What will be the next power plant to explode and meltdown? Bible Code researcher Axel Smythe finds out the hard way he should keep his mouth shut, no matter what he discovers secretly encoded in the Torah.

12. <u>Title</u>: **Predicting U.S. Presidents** [and World Leaders – All Found Torah-Encoded]; see my website, www.PredictingPresidents.com for book description.

<u>Genre</u>: political intrigue

<u>Logline</u>: scholar becomes a person of interest to major political party leaders and their money backers when he publishes discovery of all U.S. presidential election winners are identified clearly in the encoded Torah.

<u>Pitch</u>: being able to reliably predict who will be the next U.S. president becomes a matter of keen interest not only for major political parties, lobbyists, and large donors, but also for allied countries and enemies alike. Can history as reflected in the encoded Torah be influenced or changed?

<u>Description</u>: Everyone has a stake in knowing who will win the next U.S. presidential race. Much is on the line: livelihoods, power, positions of influence, wealth, reputations, and options for the future. Our independent scholar researcher reveals not only are all U. S. presidential elections found foretold in the Torah, along with the correct year and the names of all contestants, but his discovery of two search result factors for each election indicate with 100% accuracy who the winner was, or will be.

He convinces a Bible Code review board of rabbis, and they announce his break-through discovery to a skeptical and preoccupied world, which ignores the implications until the candidate selection process breaks down and presents an intolerable choice to a fed-up electorate.

Can he dig deeper and come up with alternate candidate names? Can they be persuaded to run? Can he find assassination in the coded mix, and can that be arranged in conformity to what is Torah-encoded, in order to save the country from electoral disaster, social collapse, and economic ruin?

13. <u>Title</u>: **Saving Russia** (or "To Save Russia")

<u>Genre</u>: historical political thriller

<u>Logline</u>: reversing Russia's implosion and geopolitical reversion to historically based paranoia becomes the West's strategy to avoid war.

<u>Pitch</u>: if Russia's decline can be reversed, war might be avoided.

<u>Rationale</u>: What Russia needs to reverse its negative trends: undo the kleptocracy (Putin rationed out the country's assets to his friends); equitably redistribute control of companies and industries; encourage foreign investment; rationalize and capitalize banks (with help from the U.S. Federal Reserve); diversify industries so economy is not so dependent on oil; provide incentives for young, educated people to make lives for themselves, including starting small businesses; stabilize and slowly increase the population through marriage and family counseling (in which apply the "Five Love Languages" insights of Gary Chapman) to strengthen bonds of pairing for love that lasts ("... for only love can make the fallen angel rise, in a pair of two to paradise" – line from movie *Fallen Angel* (1945), spoken by Alice Faye to Dana Andrews as he's falling asleep while they lie on the bed); financial rewards for getting married and having children; since abortion is the main form of 'birth control' in Russia, greatly increase quality and number of well-funded foster parents, so children at least have a chance at a good life; decrease alcohol consumption through mandatory counseling and treatment programs.

How to reassure Russia the West does not want and does not plan to attack it? From the Russian perspective, that is exactly where the next military attack will come from, if history is any guide. Over the centuries Russia has been attacked by European countries. Whether it was France's

Napoleon, or Germany's Kaiser in WW I or Hitler in WW II, Russia has been attacked and invaded by the most powerful armies in Europe, and suffered tens of millions of lives lost. Moscow is determined that will never happen again. The fact the the EU and NATO have official compacts of non-aggression, they see Russia asserting its natural right to its historical sphere of influence as belligerence and aggression. Moscow is just trying to discourage, and preempt if necessary, the next attack from the West on the Motherland.

While most people think of Russia as a European country, it spans the continent of Asia to the peninsula of Europe. The Urals is thought to arbitrarily divide Europe from Asia, but European civilization did not penetrate to the Urals, its bedrock cultural institutions having stopped their influences at the western border of Russia. It also is not European culturally, not having lived through the Enlightenment or the Reformation. It has never been long without a dictator, so liberal democracy has not been able to embed itself in the social and political fabric or norms of Russian culture.

14. <u>Title</u>: **School and Mass Shootings Code**

<u>Genre</u>: mystery-thriller

<u>Logline</u>: Stef Kanat, loner Bible Code researcher, discovers secretly encoded in the Torah all deadly school and mass shootings worldwide, including the full names of those killed, and the names of the perpetrators, and the weapons they used

<u>Pitch</u>: When the researcher finds his own daughter's name encoded in a horrific school shooting Torah Matrix (of an event yet to occur), what can he do to undo fate and fight the dictates of destiny revealed in the sacred, ancient text? Is there anything he can do to save her, and the other children found named in this Code of Destiny?

<u>Description</u>: [Direct reference to my Torah Code searches can be shown as part of scenes illustrating motivation of the main character, Stef Kanat, Bible Code researcher; see my 2013 book *Death's Bible Code*, Part 4, pp.16-28: Aurora movie theater, Colorado; Columbine High School; Kent State Univ., Ohio; Sandy Hook Elementary School, Newtown, Conn.; Santa Monica College, Calif.; Tucson, Arizona].

He finds encoded in the Torah all deadly school and mass shootings worldwide, including the U.S., Germany, and Russia. The Code search Matrix printout includes thelocation, the victims' names, the name of the shooter, the weapon(s) used, and the date(or at least the correct year)   quite a feat of encoding for a large text of 304,805 Hebrew letters, the Five Books of Moses, that is about 3400 years old. According to researchers, the NSA concluded that we today do not have the computing or encoding power to accomplish such a feat (see J. Satinover, 1977, *Cracking the Bible Code*).

Stef Kanat and others wonder if not only the past is revealed hidden in the sacred text, but if the future can also be uncovered using the same detection method, or an inventive variation of it.

He finds his own daughter's name encoded in the multi-linked way that shows near historical certainty. If he wants to succeed in saving her he'll need to figure out how to defeat time itself, and avoid a paradox if he can stop her death from occurring in the circumstances described in the Bible Code Matrix where her name so clearly appears. Heart-broken and in a near panic he proceeds at full speed until the appointed time, holding on to desperate hope that he can save her and other children.

15. Title: **Store the Heat, Save the Planet**

Genre: adventure political thriller

Logline: modulate global warming, and save the planet – if an adequate heat-sink can be found or developed, excess atmospheric heat could be stored, thus lowering average planetary surface temperature, defeating global warming.

Pitch: today's concern about a critical factor affecting human survival potential, excessive planetary heat which alters the environment perhaps to a non-reversible point, needs a long-term solution.

Premise: during this inter-glacial, planetary warming cycle, we should find ways to store the excess heat (in a "heat-sink") so we can use it later, when the next ice age starts. The coming ice age will kill millions of people if no way is found to moderate it, and cause massive migration and destruction of habitat, ecology, infrastructure and economies. Like the Pentagon says: "Global warming, or climate change, is a national security matter."

The most recent ice age, called "The Mini Ice Age" occurred around the 18th century and affected northern and central Europe, drastically altering societies in those regions.

Description: a rogue geologist proposes a heat-sink for the excess heat disturbing the ecological equilibrium of the Earth. When he demonstrates its effectiveness and effici-ency, he is faced with the resistance of vested interests who have invested hugely in the prospect of global warming and its consequences. The small start-up he works with developing his invention is investigated by the IRS and the Commerce Department, halting its growth and viability as a business, putting an end to his prospects for helping to heal the planet.

Turnaround comes with two billionaire brothers investing in a <u>new</u> start-up, where he is given free reign to further develop and perfect his proposal. His marketing is resisted by mainstream science and media, but is overcome by his super-rich sponsors who are determined to break the stranglehold Congress has on regulatory repression of innovation.

Start of breakthrough comes with public demonstration of utility and effectiveness of his high-tech heat-sink. More backers line up, stock soars, and international con-tracts for production and distribution are signed. Celebrations ensue, and prospects for planetary salvation look brighter. The race is on to beat heat increase to the no-return point and equalize in time for an eventual reversal to at least temporary equilibrium.

16. <u>Title</u>: **Train Crash Code**

<u>Genre</u>: political intrigue

<u>Logline</u>: government rail safety officials around the world are interested in the researcher's tested and credible claim he has uncovered buried deep in an ancient sacred text that is the basis for the Hebrew religion the history of train wrecks, where and when they occurred, and who died if the accident was deadly, with their full names found encoded in the text close to the details of the train accident itself.

<u>Pitch</u>: Can train wrecks be predicted by the researcher who discovered all train crashes encoded in the Torah? Can he be made to cooperate in improving rail safety world-wide? Or will he be persecuted as a type of witch who could have stopped the accidents, and maybe even cooperated with others who actually <u>caused</u> the accidents? All train wrecks are found clearly encoded in the Torah from Numbers 8:17 to Deuteronomy 10:8; skipping 324 letters to find the Key, "train crash," encoded (phonetically transliterated from English letter sounds to Hebrew letters, since the computer program *Bible Code Plus* can be searched only with Hebrew letters and words).

<u>Description</u>: Beyond the political aspect of government officials improving their standing with respective electorates, there is the financial and economic impact that improving rail safety generally would have on a nation's growth prospects. Elected officials want to stay in office, and increasing rail safety, efficiency and profitability is one way to help them do that.

More than public safety is at stake – political careers are on the line once it is learned that it might be possible to *predict* and thus possibly avoid trains from crashing and causing all sorts of damage, pollution, environmental contamination, and injury.

Our scholar loner hero researcher unavoidably gets in the middle of those cross cur-rents of power, and suffers for it as competing interests don't necessarily see eye-to-eye on what's best for the public versus business profits and the bottom line, compared to the damage and costs, even in human life, of train crashes.

17. <u>Title</u>: **Tsunami Code**

<u>Genre</u>: mystery-thriller

<u>Logline</u>: researcher meets resistance as he tries to save lives by predicting tsunamis, after finding them encoded in the Torah, along with their locations and dates, and victims' names encoded.

<u>Pitch</u>: death and destruction from tsunamis can be avoided if we could only predict where and when they will strike. Our hero does just that, but in a way not immediately accepted, so he has to fight against vested interests and convince at least <u>some</u> of them to give his predictive model a chance.

Description: rogue Bible Code researcher Stef Kanat discovers the history of deadly tsunamis are encoded in the Torah, the Five Books of Moses, from Genesis 8:11 to Joshua 13:14 (skipping 16,073 letters to find the Key, 'tsunami,' encoded, as transliterated into English using sounds of corresponding Hebrew letters).

He tries to develop a predictive model and has an oceanographic researcher, after much resistance and ridicule, agree to test it worldwide in real time, When enough of his 'predictions' come true, real interest is generated in what becomes accepted as a proven theory applicable to the attempt to save lives and property by providing adequate warning to vulnerable populations and communities.

18. Title: **War Deaths' Code**

Genre: mystery-thriller

Logline: implications for the Bible Code researcher who discloses his discovery of finding all war dead names Torah-encoded, along with the name of the war in which they died, turn dangerous for him and his team.

Pitch: name the war and you'll find it encoded in the Torah. Name those who died in those wars and you'll find their names encoded in exactly the same part of the Torah. This revelation frightens a lot of people and the researcher who disclosed it has a hard time living down the exposure.

Rationale: (see my 2013 book *Death's Bible Code*, Part 7, pp. 55-63; U.S. Wars – Afghanistan, Gulf War, Iraq War: 'Desert Storm,' Vietnam).

Description: implications for Bible Code researcher Stef Kanat, who discloses his discovery, turn dangerous for him and his team. People don't like to know their fate is already findable in black and white in an ancient, sacred text. Disbelief and resistance run rampant as his discovery is rejected in many quarters.

He persists in giving demonstration lectures, fully illustrated with Torah Matrices, allowing audiences to participate and ask questions, as he slowly overcomes public wariness about the disturbing implications, such that our fates are sealed and we apparently have no free choice or will.

His talks to vets groups, while troubling for them as they try to adjust their world view to incorporate such a radical view of fate, that it can be uncovered in a sacred text, explains some mysterious things about this world and its relation to the ultimate composer of the Torah.

He is finally hailed as contributing to a healing process of coming to terms with death, and honored for his efforts to put an end to war.

19. <u>Title</u>: **WW II A-Bombs' Code**

<u>Genre</u>: historical political thriller

<u>Logline</u>: A-bombings of Hiroshima and Nagasaki are found Torah-encoded, putting our hero, loner researcher in hot water with all sorts of authorities and agencies.

<u>Pitch</u>: What could discovering the A-bombing of Japan near the end of WW II encoded in the Torah have to do with current military policy? Can such research be used to uncover secret Pentagon or other governments' plans? Can the Code of Destiny be altered to help ensure a more peaceful future?

<u>Premise</u>: see my 2013 book *Death's Bible Code*, Part 8, "WW II City Bombings," pp.64-69, 'Hiroshima' as Key (found encoded from Exodus 9:21 to Leviticus 11:6; skip 3274 letters to find the Key encoded); 'Nagasaki' as Key (found encoded from Genesis 1:1 to Deuteronomy 16:22; skip 14,119 letters); partial search results; see book for more. Many aspects of the bombings are found encoded, including the precise dates, pilots' names, the planes' nicknames, and type (B-29), and the names of the A-bombs dropped ("Fat Man," and "Little Boy"), and the island from which the bombers flew, 'Tinian,' and the target country (Hebrew for 'Japan,' 'Jpn'), and the nature of the bomb ('uranium,' and '(a)tomic,' and 'weapon').

<u>Description</u>: what does the Code of Destiny reveal about what we can't avoid? Stef Kanat, loner Bible Code researcher, tries to answer these troubling questions, and others, asked of him by government agents intent on uncovering what he can discover about the future as revealed in his closely held investigative results as he probes deeper into a cosmic code buried in the ancient, sacred text of the Hebrew Torah.

Five more movie proposals and partial treatments (added on Dec 12-17, 2016, and on January 15, 2017; that is initial typing, and then expanded texts):

1: <u>Title</u>: DIRTY BOMB SCHOOL BUSES

<u>Genre</u>: Terror thriller

<u>Logline</u>: old school buses are used as dirty bombs to bring a nation to its knees.

<u>Pitch</u>: Out-of-service, surplus, old school buses are bought up around the country by terror front groups, refurbished, and loaded with fertilizer and oil (modeled after the Oklahoma City truck bomb), and stolen radioactive medical waste, to make a "dirty bomb," that will contaminate swaths of major city downtowns, thus crippling the national economy.

<u>Description</u>: In a dozen U.S. cities, used, refurbished school buses are outfitted with a ton of fertilizer, oil, and radioactive medical waste stolen from hospitals and medical clinics. Instead of suicide bombers, the buses are equipped with remote control detonators.

Coordinated detonations set off a nationwide panic as large areas of each down-town are contaminated and ruled uninhabitable for months while clean-up is attempted. The economic impact causes a recession and massive unemployment, straining state budgets, roiling financial and stock markets on Wall Street and internationally.

Follow-on attacks in suburban malls across the country cause further turmoil, chaos and hardship, overwhelming some police, ambulance services and hospitals.

2: <u>Title</u>: ELECTION REPAIR: "Hillary 2020 – How She Can Win"

<u>Genre</u>: Political drama

<u>Logline</u>: Relocating excess voters to other states could ensure Democrat party presidential wins in the foreseeable future.

<u>Pitch</u>: Billionaire(s) finances strategy to help ensure Democrat party presidential victory in Electoral College in every election from now on.

<u>Premise-Scenario</u>: A George Soros type billionaire finances the relocation of Democrat party voters (and their willing family members, when needed), the numbers of which were not needed to win any particular state for the Dems.

Spreading around these "excess" voters to precincts in other states lost in the prior election would help ensure the number of votes to secure a win there and thus that many more Electoral College votes.

A post-election examination of the 2016 presidential election showed Hillary Clinton won the popular vote by about 2.8 million votes, and lost the Electoral College vote (not getting the required 270 minimum), because many "excess" votes in certain states, such as California, New York and Illinois, were **not needed** for her to win there; they were just "added" votes on top of the 51% needed to win those states.

If many of those "excess" voters could be convinced and somehow incentivized to relocate to another state where Hillary fell just short of winning, and push the Democrat numbers up above 50%, then that state and others would bring the next Dem candidate over the top to win in the Electoral College, and thus be president.

Keeping abreast of the demographic and party affiliations on a precinct basis, and adjusting the voter relocation program accordingly would help ensure a perpetual Democrat win for president.

The same effort could be done at the level of counties for Senate and House seats in the <u>state</u> legislatures, <u>and</u> for the two houses of Congress in Washington, swinging <u>all</u> elections in the Democrat party favor.

Given the persistent nationwide numerical and Electoral College Dem party advantage – they start out with more registered voters and more states than the Republicans – what can the Repubs do to counter such a socio-political engineering effort? It doesn't amount to directly <u>buying votes</u>, but only spreads vetted, committed Dem voters around so their numbers are more effectively used as votes on the ground where they would actually make a difference in the overall outcome.

How can such an effort be countered effectively? Assuming the Dem candidate is not as flawed as Hillary was (both in 2008 against party rival Barack to whom she lost the Dem party nomination, and against DJ Trump in 2016; surely her last hurrah), how can the Republican party distribute its advantages to winning effect in 2018, 2020, 2022, and 2024?

Will the populist and nationalist appeal burn themselves out in the reality of entrenched Dem regulations weighing down the economy, and not allow the turn- around hoped for even by the Dems who crossed over and voted for Trump?

Of course, turnabout is fair play, so the Repubs and the billionaire(s) who back them, could finance such a plan to relocate die-hard Repub voters to precincts where they are most needed to turn an election (at whatever level, local, county, state, or national) to the party's favor.

Dialogue in various scenes of strategy meetings of Democrat Party operatives (to be populated by characters fleshed out in the actual film script):

"Trump won the election in the 'blue wall' states by a total of about 80,000 votes, in the northern tier of states that he surprisingly won, Wisconsin, Ohio, Michigan, and Pennsylvania. Minnesota and Illinois went for Hillary in enough numbers to swing them for the Democrats."

"Right, so you see how such a program as we suggest, of relocating the balancing numbers of Democrats to these and other close states, could impact the outcome."

"Doing the next election with last election's data, coupled with updated polling and in-field demographics, could give us enough of a picture to project with time to spare the numbers we need to relocate to certain key states. All they need to do is comply with residency requirements, if any, and register to vote in a timely way, and show up at the polls or vote absentee."

"The Electoral College was set up in 1787, and was a way to avoid the tyranny of the majority, and was meant to include all of the states, and all the people. That's exactly the structure we need to convince the electorate we believe in and trust."

"Hillary won the popular vote by about 2.8 million votes. She won California by 4.3 million, so moving about 4 million of those voters to other states, where they were needed, would help ensure Democrat party dominance for every presidential election to come, and for other elections too, such as senator and in the House."

"Catholics, and college-educated men went for Trump in unprecedented numbers. Other than broadening our appeal, raw numbers can overwhelm the populist appeal stirred up by the right, or whatever core constituency we can describe as Trump supporters."

"In the Wisconsin recount, Trump gained 131 votes. In the Electoral College, Hillary lost more votes than Trump in the final tally. All the hype in the media, first about her inevitable win, and about his lack of qualifications as president, unnecessary hostility of the press toward Trump, then the hype of recounts, then the hype of a possible rogue Electoral College, all in service to an inability to process the shock of losing so badly to Trump, an outsider, and to the Republicans across the board."

"Not to change the subject, but regarding the Russian interference, which amounted to informing the American electorate of things we did not want them to be aware of about our party and those who still run it, we must not forget that the U.S. has intervened in foreign elections 80 times since 1946, so its hands are not clean on that score. Advantaging national interests is the point, so we can recognize the *real polik* dynamics when the Russians do it, or anyone else."

"On the question of who can vote in the first place, other than illegals who need only what's called a three-pack, available on any street corner in for example Los Angeles, a fake driver's license, a fake social security card and a fake residency permit for work, all for about $150..."

"Not only don't we know how many illegals vote in every election, some say up to five percent of the turnout is of illegals, which is surely enough to turn most races, but in some states felons are allowed to vote, for example in Maine and Vermont, where prisoners are also allowed to vote."

"Yes indeed, that would be another way to increase the vote turnout, so to speak. In states that don't allow felons or ex-felons to vote, such as Florida, election results could be strongly affected if we could get that law changed. For example, 25% of Florida's black population is disenfranchised by way of convicted felon status –that's a million potential voters who would vote overwhelmingly Democrat."

"So a multi-state campaign of challenging laws to allow ex-felons, and even prisoners, to vote, would add to the natural Democrat party advantage, thus shoring up the goal of perpetual Democrat rule."

"As they say, 'you can't beat somebody with nobody,' so adding bodies on the ground who are viable voters will help ensure victory. And as you know, there is no substitute for victory."

"War demands sacrifices, and some of those bodies will fall by the wayside, one way or the other."

"What do you mean, 'war'?"

"If you don't think war is being waged against us, how do you think such massive, continent-wide losses to Republicans, at all levels of governing, occurred?"

"Yes, of course, everyone knows politics is war. What I meant is what form of warfare is politics for <u>you</u>."

"It's the no-cost-barred, bare knuckle, drag-out type. Is that clear enough for you?"

"Crystal, but you know me, I always want to make everything about <u>you</u>."

"Touching. Now can we please get back on point?"

"It wasn't warfare. The landscape had shifted under our feet and we thought demography, class warfare and identity politics would again come through for us, as we continued to believe in 'the stupidity of the American voter,' as our architect of Obamacare, the ACA, put it, would continue to prevail in keeping us in power."

"Did Bernie Sanders hurt Hillary so much she couldn't recover from the damage? And radical Elizabeth Warren harping from the Left kept her on the defensive, and not able to move to the center, as Bill did in his two elections and governing."

"Not even the Pope could defeat Trump, stating as his Holiness did his opposition to the idea of what amounted to controlled borders, with his so-called 'compassion'."

"The Dem party leadership is urging Democrats Trump has named as possible administration or cabinet picks not to accept the offer … putting party over country."

"When we run out of excuses for her why she lost, we can always start blaming the Russians. They always make a convenient punching bag and scapegoat."

"So, have we learned our lesson?"

"I doubt it, as the Russian-hacked and leaked emails of the Democratic National Committee revealed. Back-stabbing, cheating by providing Hillary with debate questions against Bernie Sanders, racism, and anti-Semitism are alive and well in our party and among its top leaders. The American electorate did not need to see that, but the Russians made sure they did. That's called intervening in an election. And it needs to stop."

"So we deserved to get creamed, is that what you're saying?"

"If the condom fits, wear it. You can interpret it any way you want. I'm just trying to figure out why we lost in such a big way and are now out of power at all levels of government and across the board."

"It does seem to have been more than just a 'change' election. It feels like something even more fundamental than that. Dems lost 1030 seats across the country during Obama's two terms, including governorships."

"You're right. We thought we had our finger on the pulse of the people, but what we sensed only amounted to hearing an echo of our wishful thinking inside the echo chamber bubble we've lived in for decades now."

"The question is, will these defeats motivate us enough to change course in a new direction? Not yet, apparently, what with Nancy Pelosi's crew still in charge, and a Minnesota Muslim leader who advocated a separate country for American blacks up for speaker of the House."

"Look, we've got to admit it, Hillary was a flawed candidate and a bad campaigner, spending one point three billion bucks of the two billion in the war chest, and not even campaigning in Wisconsin or other parts of the so-called Blue Wall."

"We're still thrashing around for a real reason for why she lost, but most of the public knows we're just looking for excuses or just making them up. The recounts didn't work, trying to sway members of the Electoral College didn't work, and now claims of Russia hacking the actual voting tallies aren't working, but the CIA leaked addendum to their report on *Kompromot* is sticking to the wall. Filthy but effective in how it worms into public consciousness through the sheer force of repetition in the media. No matter how many qualifiers they attach to its discussion, terms like 'un- substantiated' stop carrying any weight after a while. Salacious wins every time."

"Like in the 1950s when the KGB planted in the U.S. press, through their agents in place throughout the media, the fake story of FBI chief J. Edgar Hoover liking to wear women's clothing in private. That story is no longer questioned or doubted, buried so deep in the American mind it can't even be challenged. That's an example of how effective the Russians can be."

"And now we have Representative John Lewis of Georgia, a black civil rights leader with a long history of protesting, stating publicly he is convinced, because of so-called Russian hacking of the election, that Trump is not a legitimate president. He said this five days before the inauguration. How irresponsible can you get?"

"Right, the hacking has not been shown to have changed even one vote directly. It was the Hillary emails released to Wikileaks that might have changed people's minds. But since she got about 2.8 million more votes than Trump, it looks like any effort they made in that direction failed miserably. And there is no hacking scenario of perhaps targeting the Blue Wall states that turned the Electoral College vote total so far in his direction that would be credible. He ended up with 304 total."

"Even on election night, exit polls across the country had her winning. Of course we're all in shock. No wonder we've searched through a menu of reasonable explanations for her loss, from having some key recounts done, to Comey's FBI faux investigation into her classified emails, to Russian hacking, to pressuring some Electoral College members to change their vote, to claiming a downright illegitimate process that invalidates his presidency."

"We've got to grow up and get over this or people will start to see through us and the party and its platform. It's dangerous, and we'd better wake up quick or the party is over, in more ways than one."

"Yes, we went for the popular vote strategy, and assumed the Electoral College votes of the Blue Wall states in the rust belt would hold firm, even though she didn't really campaign there."

"Right, and it almost worked. The total vote difference in the three Blue Wall states totaled about 76,000 votes. So this new George Soros plan to transport and transplant enough Democrat voters would have worked in those key states to carry the day and win her the election, if only we had thought of it earlier."

"Of course it's a numbers game, so we'll need to calibrate projections of what numbers are called for and move ahead with the Soros relocation campaign. Enough newly transplanted Dem voters in the right counties will most likely do it."

"We all agree, don't we, that these people can't be random characters picked up and dropped into a community willy-nilly? They have to be carefully chosen and screened for good cultural, ethnic, education and income fit. We can hire a Sociologist to set up the vetting criteria and assignment protocols, selecting the right individuals for relocation, along with the best family composition and skill sets for employment."

"Again, the inauguration day massive protest marches against Trump across the country were so frustrating. Surveys showed a large proportion of those marchers were not even registered to vote or did not vote. Many said they were so confident that Hillary would win, as every expert and media outlet predicted, they felt no urgency or real need. They felt Trump was a fool who could not possibly win."

"Maybe next time, no matter who the Republicans put up, they won't be so damn cocky. We can't afford such a mistake again, especially in the face of losing so many races across the state levels of government in so many states."

"So our fallback immediate position is no honeymoon of any kind for this new president. I don't care how traditional it is to allow what usually has been a seven month honeymoon period. We can't afford one for this clown, he's a danger and threat to the country."

"With the added leverage of felons released and allowed to vote under the new law, will help us too. They'll see which side their bread is buttered on."

"Much less the millions of illegals who can vote undetected with identification documents bought on any downtown street corner for about $125. Those votes are undetectable as illegal, because registration even when a driver's license is required, is above board and appears perfectly normal."

"If this demographic vote distribution management program, funded by our billionaire supporters, doesn't pan out, we're cooked, and for more than only one generation too."

"In mid-January Nancy Pelosi, still leading the party in the House, blamed Bush for Obama's enormous, record-breaking national debt, the largest in history under one president. She's not fooling anybody, so why does she keep up this foolishness?"

"Maybe it's helping convince even more Democrats to boycott Trump's inauguration. Sixty-eight House members, almost all minorities, including the one illegal alien elected to the House, have announced they won't be there. Even more are lining up to stay away. And pressure on performers who said they'd entertain the crowd of the expected seven hundred thousand are dropping out almost daily."

"About one hundred protest groups have applied for permits for that day, so it should be quite a party."

[dejected and defeated and doubtful looks all around, some shaking their heads]

"Trump's Flynn fiasco twenty four days into his term was only a sign of what was to come, what with the calls for investigations. General Flynn as his national security adviser choice was tainted by Russia well before he chose him. We might never know fully why he so favored Russia in all parts of his perspective, but we do know his phone calls prior to Trump's inauguration to the Russian ambassador assuring him that any Obama sanctions slapped on due to Moscow's interference in the election would soon be lifted, was ill-advised."

"The Justice Department was notified by the intelligence agency who intercepted the phone call, being tasked to monitor all foreign phone calls, nineteen days prior to Flynn's resignation or firing. So potentially Trump knew of the problem for almost three weeks before taking action. The impression is that they thought they could keep it quite and cover it up. Big mistake."

"The problem was he apparently lied to Pence the VP. Trump didn't need any Russian help in order to win. The Republican party destroyed itself in the process of his winning. He beat the best field of contestants they could ever mount, over a dozen well qualified people who in any other period would have successfully appealed, other than in the aftermath of Obama and the deep anger he created in much of the American electorate, at least in the key states where votes really mattered."

"Hillary won the popular vote by almost three million nationally, and actually came fairly close in the Blue Wall states she assumed would hold. A tweak in strategy and a shift in campaign timing and speaking appearances could have tipped her over the top in the Electoral College. Or not, depending on Trump's true degree of appeal."

"But you're not suggesting, are you, that tweaking her 2020 run in that way would prove adequate, are you?"

"No, I think we all realize a complete revamp is called for. We know she's an appealing and sympathetic candidate, although admittedly not the best campaigner."

"Are you suggesting the third time could be the charm? In 2008 she ran into the buzz-saw out of left field in the form of an unknown, new Senator from Illinois named Obama, and she lost the nomination. And in 2016 was able to get the nomination, barely, after a 74-year-old Socialist from Vermont almost beat her for the party's nod. And then lost to Trump. What makes you think a third run, in 2020, would end up any differently, even with your so-called tweaking of strategy?"

"If we use the best, up to date data in the Blue Wall states and in other states that were also fairly close, we have time to shape the demography in her favor, by trans-planting enough Democrat party voters from states where they're not needed to win, the so-called 'excess voters,' in states like California, Illinois and New York, and settle them in the right districts in those key, close states, to ensure they swing her way. I guarantee the outcome, at least to the extent that anything can be guaranteed in politics."

"As to how to incentivize them, that social psychologist I told you about can take care of the planning for that. Relocating will involve job referrals and housing arrangements, stipends and subsidies for living expenses, transportation, food, clothing, and everyday expenses. Setting up a new life in a compatible neighborhood."

"I'm telling you, this does look like a sure bet. A vote is a vote is a vote, and we best not allow too many be wasted where they are in excess and not actually needed to win. And winning is the point, after all. Spread them around to where they are actually needed, and we have a sure-fire formula for victory in the Electoral College."

"So you're saying this time she could actually win, not just win in all the polls prior to the election, like in 2016, and then actually lose, but win at least the minimum number of needed Electoral College votes, 270, and actually be president, the first woman president in American history. Now that's worth fighting for!"

"Yes, that's exactly what I'm saying, and it's not based on wishful thinking, like was done in her past campaigns. We've laid out the basic strategy for accomplishing it. It's a bit time-consuming vetting the voters and funding those willing to relocate and establish a new life for themselves in a new state, but the aggregate numbers, as you've seen in the county-by-county analysis of how moving in these new voters alters the projected results enough to swing the states for her."

"By the way, some of those Democrat voters contacted for possible relocation could very well have family members in those states who they would like to be close to once again. That sort of family link is worth exploring as a data point as we look at the collated voter rolls."

"We can build in a margin of safety in the numbers by relocating more Democrat voters than we need to win, just in case the Republicans catch on to our ploy and try to counter our moves to build up the voter rolls. If we're quiet about it they won't have time to respond in ways to neutralize our advantage. We have the basic numbers, and there's nothing they can do about it. Numerical advantage is everything, as long as we effectively spread them around correctly, and go for the big prize in a way that can actually work and be successful in her gaining the presidency. That's the point."

"Yes, and this time Hillary will be running against Trump, assuming he doesn't get impeached and has to leave office, with the record of his first term. Why wouldn't that be to her advantage? Look at the disasters of his term so far. What a mess. All she has to do is play it cool, calmly point out his defects, and appeal not only to her faithful base but to those dissatisfied with Trump and his follies, his antics and his harmful policies. He keeps embarrassing the country. He's like an ignorant bull in a well-staffed china shop, causing more and more damage almost every day. She'll have a hell of a time cleaning up the mess. Talk about a re-set button with Russia, she'll need to straighten out all relations with the world and assure it America has not gone absolutely nuts."

"Why do you say she needs to play it cool?'

"Because both of her runs showed the more exposure she gets, the less people like her, that's why. That's not a criticism of her personally, it's just a matter of how people react to her persona and style. So she has to stay calm, be the adult in the room, and appeal to the concerns of the middle class. Her base is with her, so she doesn't need to campaign from the left so much. So screaming and yelling in a shrill voice is unnecessary to get their attention to convince them. It just turns everyone else off."

"High level Trump aides were in constant touch with senior Russian officials during the 2016 campaign. The concern is about what policy discussions occurred. The only way to get to the bottom of it is to determine under what circumstances would these personnel need to be in such constant contact. General Flynn would not reveal how much Russian Tv paid him in Moscow at the conference he attended."

"Trump's pro-Russian stance is not only revealed through his bro-mance with Vladimir Putin, but also in his refusing to criticize Russia for any of its aggressive actions, including taking Crimea and invading Ukraine. This is a problem for observers who are trying to make sense of Trump's foreign policy. Drawing a moral equivalency between Putin's murder of his opponents and journalists, and the U.S., as he did to Bill O'Reilly during his Super Bowl interview, was beyond the pale."

"He's more of an instinctive reactor than a studious, informed actor steeped in knowledge of history, diplomacy or international relations. That's the trouble, his instincts mislead him, and the country is in trouble because of it."

"Russia tested, in early February 2017, a new, nuclear-capable cruise missile, in violation of the 1987 SALT treaty. And has a spy ship, the Victor Leonov, off the coast of Maryland, and patrolling north and south about thirty miles off shore. What are they up to? No one knows for sure."

"Hillary will need to pick up the pieces, and try to fix the damage caused by his irresponsible attitude. She'll need a lot of help, but first we need to get her elected, and we think we've figured out how to practically guarantee that. Not like in 2016 when hope and media and polling bias out-paced facts on the ground, and misled everyone. Indulging in wishful thinking is not a winning strategy, as we learned the hard way in the 2016 election. Not in 2020. The blinders are off, and it's time for hard ball and the real deal. We will not lose again, or I'll quit this game."

"Don't do that, we need you. We ran this strategy by the legal department, and they're OK with it. It doesn't violate any election laws or campaign rules that they could find."

"Our billionaire supporters are willing to go beyond just campaign funding and check-book support. They're stepping up big time and putting real money into an effective strategy for her to win."

"Actually not necessarily her, depending on her health, and willingness to run again and go through all that strain and pressure, but any viable, appealing party candidate that makes it through the nomination process."

"Against a reasonable and appealing Republican like Paul Ryan, we would have a bigger problem, in case Trump doesn't run for a second term, but the same, basic voter allocation strategy would apply, and the Electoral College win can be locked in with the right voter relocation pattern."

"That's the game. We play it. To win. I didn't make up the rules."

"Someday they'll make a Broadway production, and call it 'Hillary 2020, the Musical'."

"I'd go see that."

"No, I'm saying that's a good idea. Who do we know on Broadway who could produce it? Before the election."

"It would take too long to mount. I mean, the lead time to November 2020 isn't enough to have the election effect we need. I don't think it would."

"Wrong. People will buy into the romance of it. That alone could be enough to infuse a Camelot-like aura into the collectivist proposals that would soften them enough so they go down like pleasant nostalgia. That would definitely appeal."

"You mean, like a comforting set of assurances people could believe in, compared to the hyperbole crap spewed and peddled by Clown Trump."

"One of the scenes in the musical could go like this – a boxing ring and a big crowd eagerly waiting for the heavy weight fight to begin, the main attraction of the night. The announcer yells into the mic, *'Are you ready to rumble?!'* The crowd goes wild. *'We have a doozy of a wingding for you folks tonight, like you've never seen in your lives, I guarantee! … Here we go folks … In the blue corner we have, at five feet two and weighing in at a hundred and eighty pounds, the Secretary and Senator herself, Hillary Rodham 'What Difference at This Point Does it Make' …Clinton!'*"

"The crowd goes wild, stomping and screaming, on their feet applauding. He quiets them down, and then says, *'And in the red corner, we have, at six feet two, and weighing in at three hundred pounds, the multi-billionaire president himself, Don-ald, John, 'Grab 'Em By The Pussy,' … Tru-ump!'*"

"The crowd erupts in cheers and jeers and boos and applause and cat-calls, stomping and screaming … out of control … fist fights break out, and a riot is about to explode, when the announcer screams at full volume, *'Are you ready to rumble?!'*"

"The crowd changes focus, cheering for the fight to start. Everyone is looking forward to blood in the ring and some teeth knocked out. It'll be a fight for the ages."

"I promise you this … Trump will be the last Republican president. I guarantee it. Not because he's a blustering, incoherent buffoon who thinks he can transfer business principles to national politics and survive. Any candidate that party puts up for the White House is in for a world of election hurt with this voter relocation plan. Like moving the right pawns in the right way on the chess board can stymie a queen gambit attack, and even a Sicilian bishop assault, we can arrange all our pieces so the opposition has no path to victory. None, no matter what they do. We've got the numbers and they don't. If we're smart about how we use those numbers, we win, and keep winning as long as we manage the ground game in the way I described."

"I agree, even the cross-over vote won't be enough to counter this plan. Realism will intrude on Republican optimism when they grasp the potential effects of our voter resettlement strategy on the inevitable voting outcome. Their doom is contained in our reallocation of bodies on the ground called Democrat voters outnumbering their voters. It'll be a wake-up call they won't be able to react to in time. There is no effective response they can muster, even if they move around some of their trusted voters. Their numbers don't add up, while our numbers do, to a dominant majority. So we win, and they lose, and she'll be the next president of the U.S.."

"Despair is a narcotic, it lulls the mind into monotony. At least that's about what Charlie Chaplin said as Monsieur Verdoux in his 1947 movie by the same name, a movie he wrote and directed."

"We can beat the bad habit of despair and recover from those across-the-board election losses in 2016 if we can figure out the right inducements, and incentives for those excess, loyal Democrat party voters who are interested in relocating for the good of the party and its presidential candidate. Filling out the needed numbers in counties where Republicans, and some others, out-voted Democrats will turn around the results in favor of Hillary in 2020. That's the plan. All we need is the research and the funding to place those willing voters, to relocate and vote in their new districts."

"What needs to be done at the earliest possible point, and we need to be serious about this question, 'cause it reveals a lack of imagination, is figure out why such a relocation plan as this wasn't thought of before, and executed, even prior to the 2016 election. If it had been, she could have won, and she would be president today if it had been devised early and adequately funded. I'm not indulging in coulda-woulda- shoulda here, but just trying to inspire more creative thinking outside the box that gets us to victory, and on the victory stand for the foreseeable future."

"In order to defeat Trump, we also need to understand him. Reading the recent book by Roger Stone, 'The Making of the President 2016 – How Donald Trump Orchestrated a Revolution,' would help. And reading Trump's book, 'The Art of the Deal,' is important to understand him as a business man, a man, and as a builder, and essentially as a deal maker. Also his book 'Crippled America,' later released as a paperback and re-titled 'Great Again – How To Fix Our Crippled America'."

"Also, it's a great sport to try and psychoanalyze Trump. Big mistake. Dr. Allen Frances, who wrote the DSM medical guidelines for doctors says that those who say Trump is mentally ill are wrong. He was a guest of Don Lemon on CNN on February 15, 2017 and said 'there's no reason to call him psychiatric names. Yes, he's impulsive, but … we have to fight his threat to democracy on political grounds, not medical grounds. Claims that he is mentally ill are absurd. He doesn't have a condition that calls for diagnosis'."

"As far as leaks are concerned and how we can exploit them to Hillary's advantage, attorney Jay Sekulow says revealing secret wiretap tapes is a felony, and such leaks here, against Trump, amounts to a soft coup, in the case for example of General Flynn talking with the Russian ambassador to the U.S., prior to him being sworn in as National Security Adviser. President Obama and the DOJ waited til Obama had seventeen days left in office to authorize from one agency to 16 other agencies the sharing of wiretap information, thus greatly expanding the problem of tracking down leaks. Which was Obama's point in actively undermining Trump's presidency. That directive will need to be reversed as soon as Hillary is sworn in."

"Such pseudo insurrections are what can destroy a revolution. Historically deviational tripe can be very appealing to the masses. Just ask Hillary, with her collectivist jargon, like 'It Takes a Village.' The proletariat eats up that crap."

"Now that the Democrats are in the wilderness, all we can do is resist and obstruct, and divert attention, apply all the Saul Alinsky tactics we can think of. Into the vacuum, the media, ninety percent Democrat, has moved as a force to fight back against Trump. They're more than the Fourth Estate, the left wing of the Establishment that is a vital part of the so-called 'swamp' that Trump says he wants to drain. Trump goes over their heads directly to the American people with his crazy tweets and ranting rallies. Why they eat it up I have no idea, but it's a political phenomenon we're going to have to get a handle on before we commit resources in an uninformed campaign of massive voter relocation. More groundwork needs to be done is all I'm saying."

"The deep state is Obama's shadow government embedded in the Washington bureaucracy. The Democrat party has been marginalized, and lost over a thousand seats and offices across the country since 2012. Undermining and sabotaging President Trump is their only option. Obama had the full spectrum of support, including the media, the press, academia, Hollywood, and the entertainment establishment. Trump has very little of that support, hardly any at all."

"If he ignores the political chattering class and focuses on his domestic agenda, he'll keep his 55% approval rating. The establishment doesn't want Trump to succeed, including some key Republicans. The public is tired of being misled, that's what he tapped into on his run for office. When Trump said the media and press are the enemy of the American people, he might have gone a bit too far, but mostly because he does not slow down and explain the connecting dots for his conclusion. Unless there is an understanding of a free and independent press, as specified in the Constitution, that is quite different from the state of the American press today. Liberals are blind to their bias. It's not free or independent of the Democrat party, it serves as a political arm of the party., so it has abdicated its Fourth Estate responsibilities. That's what he means."

"One of the last straws for many people was when the singer Madonna said at the women's march and rally in Washington, 'I have thought an awful lot about blowing up the White House.' Jodi Foster made no political or violent or hateful or dangerous statements, yet a nut like John Hinkley, in an effort, he said, to impress the actress, shot President Reagan and almost killed him. How many dangerous nut cases did Madonna set off with her inflammatory venom? Will she be happy when Melania is a widow? Does she want America to go through another presidential assassination and its devastating after-effects? Did the Secret Service interview her? Shouldn't she explain herself and apologize? Not only to that rally's organizers and sponsors, but to the nation and American people as a whole."

We follow a young, ardent Hillary supporter, Ann Crawford, 23, a recent college graduate, a statuesque blonde with nascent political ambitions of her own, through the 2016 election campaign and the aftermath in the streets erupting with anti-Trump protests. She works hard as a volunteer at the Washington, D.C. Democrat party campaign headquarters and impresses some higher-ups who happen to notice her striking beauty and dedication, and over-hear bits of her articulate arguments with staff.

In the election's aftermath of shock and dismay felt by fully everyone involved in Hillary's campaign, the organizers of a protest rally remember Ann, contact her and ask her to help setup some logistics and to facilitate communications with other rallies across the country. Ann's junior year abroad in France had created some useful contacts in Paris; in communication with some of them, some of their ideas for protests translated well for the U.S.. Those French really know how to shut down a city to make a serious point in resisting a repressive government.

Her contributions were noticed by the Election Repair group's leaders and she is asked to come aboard the coordinating committee to set up a national out-reach apparatus. Her contacts had proliferated and her data base had grown to the extent it was now a useful resource for the DNC's chair. She is finally brought in on the 'Hillary 2020' planning group. Her commitment and quick, analytical mind soon help her rise to the inner sanctum of power, where the key decisions are made on how to implement the plan to get Hillary elected in 2020. They all knew this was their chance to make that a reality. Their focus and determination come from their hearts and guts, but they let their clear heads show them the way. A way to victory is in sight. They feel it in their bones and are willing to sacrifice much to realize that dream.

"When the press aligns itself with a particular movement, in this case, liberalism and the Democrat party, the press is not free, it's adversarial against conservatives, and biased by at least ten to one in that direction, as evidenced by party and candidate contributions for example. This bias is pervasive across other institutions too, such as academic, Hollywood, the entertainment industry, the education apparatus, journalists, and even Wall Street. It might have the delusion it's independent, as specified in the Constitution, but more and more voters see through this ruse, and are getting sick of it. No wonder the public's trust in the media is so low."

"Hopefully Hillary fires all her campaign experts who ran such a losing effort that had a losing strategy. They had no idea what they were doing, and still don't get it. They're mystified by Trump's victory. Whitewashing excuses for the loss. Her former campaign manager, Robby Mook, said on a news show that the Russians hacking could have cost her the election. That sort of unsubstantiated nonsense makes you wonder if he was actually a paid opposition operative."

"The Not-My-President Day rallies of February 20, 2017, ironically held on Presidents Day, kept the resistance going, and encourages Hillary backers to keep working on her behalf."

"Disinformation and propaganda by the mainstream media is a force acting against the American people. I don't think this helps those poor people with their P.E.S.D., 'post-election-stress-disorder.' 93 percent of reporters donated to Hillary's campaign. That's not a sign of an independent press."

"And so the party, afflicted by unified thinking, keeps hoping something will actually work if it continues tinkering. Her campaign leaders are all of the same mindset, even months after the 2016 election, and incapable of breaking out of the prison of their own preconceived notions that led to such a disaster. Trump got about 62 million votes, and she got almost 65 million votes. We all know where she would be sitting today if they had played it smart and focused on 270, and not taken the upper Midwest for granted."

"Her campaign had two billion bucks to spend, and spent only one point three. Leaving seven hundred million on the table wasn't necessarily a crime, but if someone had come up with this voter transplant idea in time back then, that money could have been spent on a literal movement, not one with catchy slogans and angry chants, but one with real results where it counted, in voting tallies in key states that added up to at least 270 Electoral votes. That's called winning, and there was a path open for us we did not have the imagination to explore and shape to her advantage. Vitriol in the streets is no substitute for victory and power."

"I get it … a person is a body is a vote. Move the needed numbers of votes to the right precincts, and she wins the minimum 270 needed. Game over. Do that for every single election, re-assessing each precinct for changes and trends, and relocating the willing bodies accordingly … there's your winning gambit, whether nationally or state-wide. We win. I love the smell of victory, any time day or night. There's nothing like it. Power is the ultimate aphrodisiac there is. That's why it's so addictive."

———— ———— ———— ————

"Those who rallied in his inauguration day who did note vote or even register to vote are beyond redemption and are not worth reaching out to or educating or convincing. She should have reserved the term deplorable for them. Anyone that stupid is not who we want on our side. I don't care if they come in here or into any other campaign headquarters, they deserve no mercy.

Who's to say they're not double agents and trying to actually defeat her? That's exactly what they did, especially if they're from those states where their votes would've counted toward her national victory."

"What price victory? What price the White House? The ground shifted out from under our feet and we didn't adapt. Not only in time, but we're still not adapting in any conventional sense. We lost the white working class voters in the upper Midwest rust belt. That was the key to our defeat. Keith Ellison is the Sanders-backed candidate for the DNC chair, and Perez is the Obama-backed candidate. This shows a further leftward move of the party, further estranging it from the mainstream of the electorate. How does it help broaden our appeal with a Muslim radical left DNC chair? What kind of winning combo is that?"

"Why did the DNC tolerate such a mal-distribution of votes? Yes, the Blue Wall states surprisingly went for Trump, but whose fault was that? Obviously the polling was faulty and we should never use or believe those firms again, but our observers on the round missed the shift, until it was too late. That part of the ground game needs improvement. This new strategy corrects that problem. Trump's winning margin was not enough in those states for us now to overcome it with the adjustment we've come up with. If the ground shifts again, we can be ready for it."

"Actually, too many registered Democrats crossed over and voted for Trump. The precinct workers didn't pick up on the change in attitude and the anger rampant in the electorate. That shouldn't happen again. It can't, or we're lost forever."

"We could use an algorithm to compensate for the statistical discrepancy evidenced in 2016 and adjust our request for an appropriate number of transplant voters in order to overcome a hidden, disruptive surprise. I say, no more surprises. We can assure that by adequately covering any potential deficit. New bodies in the right districts can ensure a win. ... Hail Hillary!" [toasting]

"It's called shaping the battlefield, and flooding the zone. It's an effective way to win. There is no substitute for victory. The party lost touch with reality, but now we have to face it for them – that won't be an easy task to pull off. Ten too few votes in too many of the wrong precincts and we lose the game. I'm not about to lose this race. This is her last hoorah and I'm not gonna blow it for her. She's gonna win it this time or it's the last thing I do. I mean it."

"The roll-out is to be done quietly, not loudly in public with publicity or fanfare. It's to be a behind the scenes operation, with quiet research of voter registration rolls and confidential conversations with prospective candidates for resettlement. Word of some of what we're trying to do is bound to leak out, but no one needs to confirm or acknowledge anything. Keeping this quiet and out of the news is the best approach. Admitting to it only near when our goal is reached at saturation points in key precincts wouldn't do any harm, as long as we frame it as a social service program of helping families with a new beginning in a new location, with new opportunities for employment and good housing in safe neighborhoods with good schools."

"Hillary was right when she said, like in her book, It Takes a Village, where round pegs work with each other cooperatively and collectively to make sure no square pegs sneak into the mix, 'cause then more than micro-aggressions to occur in re-shaping them into acceptable global citizens."

"I don't think that was her main message, but I can assure you the sociologist we hired has his proprietary algorithms that pre-select the best-shaped pegs to fit right into the right precincts without arousing suspicion or causing conflict. He's a social engineering maestro with a flare for politics that's quite impressive. He's coordinating the election roll data for the right precinct fit and working with finance to facilitate a smooth transition to the transplants new neighborhoods."

"What does finance say about the cost projections? Have the sources balked at the figures of the cost per vote?

"No balking so far. We'll see what the final average bottom line expense is for each vote. My impression is there won't be any complaining, considering the total commitment expressed so far. In for a pound, in for a dollar. When these types of egos get involved, there's no stopping these guys. Not even God is gonna stop them as far as they are concerned, no matter what the Torah Code reveals. The sociologist we hired says there's a much deeper story going on having to do with the whole of human history hidden in the Torah Code, or what is popularly known as The Bible Code, a 900 year old rabbinical study discipline that this expert has explored himself and vouches for its veracity and predictive power. We can't get into it here, but believe me, its an amazing source of knowledge to explore. He has twelve books in print on his search results. I can give you the titles and his website after this meeting, if you're interested."

"Well, when the most powerful office in the world is at stake, a winning strategy that is sure-fire and flexible is absolutely irresistible to those well-heeled types who are starving to be on the winning side, and with a viable candidate who has already proven herself as a vote getter and who has already held high office and who already knows many world leaders."

"Trump first beat the Republican party, then he beat the Democrat party. Talk about a revolution, and a change election. Like Steve Bannon, adviser to Trump in the White House and on the Security Council, said, 'We need to bitch-slap the Republican party.' Bannon might not care what people think of him, but he's gonna care when Trump gets trounced by Hillary in 2020, I assure you. He's gonna care big time."

"We can't allow Trump, as his White House adviser Steve Bannon promised at the CPAC on Feb. 24, 2017, to deconstruct the administrative state. We can't allow that to happen – that has been our salvation and mainstay of support. The regulatory rollback they promise would be the death of us and must be resisted on all fronts, as the Obama bureaucrat hold-overs are doing admirably, with their leaks and their stalling."

"We can't get into the weeds here, later we can deeply explore the election results county by county in states that Hillary lost. Suffice it to say here that the map clearly shows the large number of counties in the North-East and Midwest that went for Trump over Clinton. The effect was large enough to flip the normally Democrat leaning states of Iowa, Michigan, Pennsylvania, and Wisconsin into the Republican camp. Those are our target states, and a few other close ones, for 2020."

"I realize it's dangerous to theorize in advance of facts, so we best hold off jumping to conclusions, so wallowing in our hatred of Trump misses the point of how he won, apart from the Blue Wall states falling, or the Electoral College per se, both shocks. So to undo the damage, and rectify what should have been done in 2016, this could be a voluntary movement that turns the tide of Democrat losses."

"As for claiming she could have won in 2016 using this plan, I think that's a misplaced assertion, one that doesn't take into account the basic need of the plan, data of where the deficits of voters are. Only after the election was over was there any evidence of any Democrat voter deficit in key states that could swing the election. No one questioned the Blue Wall states, and Trump seemed to have no clear path to 270, so Hillary's election was assured. All polls, surveys, journalists and experts on every channel agreed, there was no way in the world that she could lose. As the results came in late election night, I kept shouting at the television set, 'there's no way she can lose!'. I was as shocked as anyone at the final result. So for 2020, it is the results of 2016 we have to go on to devise a strategy and develop the required numbers of transplants needed in key districts in those swing states. And adjust our projections, taking into account the 2018 midterm election results in the Congressional races. If we're quick and nimble enough, we can pull this off."

"In the event the predictive model has a too-close outcome near election day, we need to have in place the list of same-day voter registration precincts so new arrivals can be moved around on an emergency basis to build up the right numbers. Last minute relocations shouldn't be a problem for people dedicated to the cause. We can expect them to willingly cooperate and do what's needed. This is an added safety measure, a safety margin designed into the project. If we're nimble enough and on top of the changing demographics and Republican voting patterns enough, we just might pull this off."

"We're a bit in the weeds here, but that's OK, it's to be expected as we ramp up. We'll need to wait for that level of detail. Some of that is the sociologist's proprietary protocol. We don't need to share it yet, but yes it's part of the path to victory. This county by county U.S. map shows how relatively few counties flipped. If we target those, it'll turn the results in 2020 to Hillary's favor. That's what we need to do."

"If there were about 76,000 votes total difference in the five Blue Wall states, and that number of Democrat voters would've turned it around … call it 85,000 to include a safety buffer, then at $10,000 per transplanted voter, that totals out at eighty five million dollars, about 12% of what Hillary's campaign left unspent in its coffers in 2016. At $5000 per transplanted voter, that's about $42.5 million dollars total, which is 6% of what she left on the table. Who would balk at that?"

"There's an update from the DNC meeting in Atlanta, where new party leaders are being chosen on February 25, 2017. Tom Perez was elected DNC chair. The take- away phrase from his acceptance speech was 'Our values are inclusion and diversity.' He's considered the most liberal of all the seven candidates. He was Obama's Labor Secretary, and worked for the Justice Department in the Civil Rights Division. He's the son of Dominican immigrants."

"Well, notwithstanding Hugh Hewitt's new book, 'The Fourth Way – The Conservative Playbook for a Lasting GOP Majority,' our strategy will upset all those assumptions and beat them where it counts, at the ballot box in an enduring pattern that will ensure our return to power and keep us there until we screw up again."

"The mystery is why she lost. Well, other than lack of imagination and planning to overcome the worse case scenario with a new, untried approach like we've developed here. Trying to answer the question of why Hillary lost in 2016, another question presents itself – why were Democrat votes so mal-distributed? Other than of course the basic demographic split between urban and rural, which does go a long way in explaining the concentration in cities of Democrat votes."

"If you're trying to point to the almost 3 million vote difference nationally in her favor, then you've put your finger on a key problem in how that vote was spread, or distributed. Not enough were in the right districts, and conversely, there were too many, that is, an excess of votes for her, in districts where she didn't need them to win those districts."

"Exactly, thus the answer presents itself. If the so-called excess votes can be moved to where they're needed, to districts she lost by rather small margins, and if the voting pattern remains relatively stable, she'll win the next election, if she chooses to run in 2020. Her presidency is all but assured if she can mount one more campaign."

"So targeting the key states where Trump won by small margins, using the resettlement strategy of committed Democrat voters, is the way to guarantee her win. It might hinge on how fickle the electorate is this time. We can compensate for that by assuming the worse case scenario of the same Republican and Democrat pattern of 2016. Enough Republicans were motivated to turn out, enough Democrats crossed over, and enough other Dems didn't bother to vote, and plenty in favor of her didn't even bother to register to vote. A deadly combination we can't count on reversing, but we can counter and overwhelm it by bringing in enough new Democrat voters from states where their votes aren't needed for her to win there. That's the resettlement plan, adding enough numbers, so there's no way the Republicans can win the key states we need to put her over the top with at least 270 Electoral College votes."

"Her loss came from two basic deficits, badly distributed votes, and leaving 700 million bucks of campaign funds on the table. Moving the bodies to where they're needed and spending the necessary money to do so would ensure her victory. She'd be in the White House today if someone had thought of this idea and taken it seriously and developed it into a viable operation that is workable on the ground. At a total cost of between 42 and 84 million dollars to relocate about 84,000 voters to the key five or six states to overwhelm the numbers she lost by in 2016 would succeed in getting her elected."

"I agree, that's worth figuring out and implementing and financing. So we're convinced we can do this. We have the team, the motivation, the vision. There is no reason not to do this. If she wants to be president, this is the ticket. We have the numbers of willing mobile voters, so this is the plan that can work to put her in the White House. That'll be a beautiful day."

"The mainstream media's intentionally wrong quotes of Trump will only turn more voters off to Democrats, because they pick it up and run with it, trying to make more political points with the base. Such as 'Whites built this country' attributed to Trump was obviously a smear he did not deserve, and voters know it. Comparing him to Hitler, Mussolini and Lenin only turns off anyone with a basic understanding of history. Calling him a fascist only ensures voters will turn out for Trump, since they know it's a false accusation. Extreme and false charges serve the cause of Republicans. Fake quotes and fake news, such as claiming Trump is planning to use 100,000 National Guard troops to round up illegals, will help him get re-elected. More and more people are seeing through the biased agenda and turning off the Trump bashing tirades. As is talk of impeachment. It'll only serve to get him re-elected and makes our task of trans- planting enough voters that much harder. That's exactly what we don't want, so the media, the press, academia, entertainers, lawyers, and wall street need to stop the discredited piling-on of faked charges and twisted quotes, or there will come a point where our relocation plans for Dem voters to where they're needed will fail to get Hillary elected."

"You're right, the misguided attitude is only digging the hole deeper. It could prove to be a fatal mistake, making it much more difficult to climb back and succeed in getting Dems elected again, in all levels of office where they were defeated all over the country. They're setting up Trump for a volley ball spike to the face, something Dems don't need, for sure."

"Those voters who are relocated are volunteer pawns in service to the Queen, pawns willing to uproot their lives and relocate to another state so she can win. I wish the DNC had thought of this and implemented it for her 2016 race, but now that they have woken up to the sweet possibilities, there's a good chance for a 2020 win."

"Let's just say that without a good matching protocol, several families could get their wires crossed, ending in not a pretty picture for anyone. They willingly volunteer and expect to improve their lives by relocating to where their votes were needed most. In the beginning, arrangements might go well in a new and exciting adventure. Things could start going south when the redneck country neighbors begin to get just a bit too suspicious of these city folk outsiders. All I'm saying is the criteria and screening and relocation choices of person and place need to be done conscientiously."

"The Republicans will continue to win if the Dems don't implement this plan of relocating Dem voters where they're most needed, to counter the deficit where she got defeated in 2016, and relieving the excess load of unneeded voters in states where she won handily. The one thing we shouldn't do is try to calibrate the winning vote margin too closely. The safety buffer referred to earlier seems at this point to be adequate, but as the race develops there might be adjustments needed, so the plan has flexibility built into it. Depending on the voter registration lead time, we'll keep track of those and move relocaters as needed when the need becomes clear."

"Something is fundamentally wrong with a political party that loses 1,049 seats and offices at all levels over the eight years of a Change president. Change is right, the destruction of the Democrat party, hollowing it out and setting it up for massive defeat across the board in 2016. Some say the party has lost touch with the American electorate. I say that doesn't matter, as long as we have enough loyal members who are willing to relocate and vote where they're need to make up for the deficit in key states."

"We've been in touch with corresponding political parties in Europe and they're very interested in our plan, particularly in how it might translate to their particular circumstances, election laws and party structure. Even Russia, China and Ukraine have inquired. They have requested to quietly observe our planning operation, and execution of the plan, its roll-out and how the results are monitored, tabulated and assessed. After the plan's results have been proven, they'd like to send representatives here for tutorials and seminars. Even the British and Australians say they want to learn how it really works and how to maximize the right effects, and how to neutralize and defeat the opposition's resistance. I'm not speaking here as an advocate, but as a strategist and a problem-solver."

"The only adequate number of needed voters we can count on to neutralize the deficit in the key states where she lost in 2016 are the transplants. A certain percentage of Democrats, whether registered to vote or not, will not vote, as we found after 2016. We can't count on those people to have learned their lesson, contributing to some degree to her defeat. So the number of needed transplanted voters need to be calculated ignoring that cohort of irresponsible voters, and compensating for them in the buffer factor mentioned earlier."

"The 16 Democrat governors up for election in 2018 will do redistricting in 2021. The relocation plan of loyal Dem voters willing to resettle and help the party in the numbers needed calculated by the algorithm mentioned earlier is crucial in setting up wins in key states in later years too. We can look beyond 2020 and use this method to secure victory at all levels for the foreseeable future."

"There have been reports that our data base and records have been hacked. I can't confirm that here, but you can be sure we are looking into it. Also, there are rumors that some pre-test transplant candidates have been identified, targeted and harassed. We're looking into those claims too, and formulating protections and privacy assurances. There might be a leak in our operation, or we're being bugged. If the problem persists or gets bigger, we'll need to take drastic measures to correct it. I'll keep you posted."

"I like our plan slogan,'Hillary 2020, a Blueprint for Victory.' Because that's exactly what it is. She would have won in 2016 with this strategy, and will win in 2020 if she gets the nomination and uses this plan in the general election. We need to explore how it might be used also by an individual candidate's campaign in the primary elections, state by state. We of course want the strongest candidate to win the nomination, to help ensure the party's victory and come-back."

"If you have excess votes over here, in other words more votes than needed to win all the Electoral College votes for that state, and you have a deficit of voters over there, how would you suggest that problem be corrected? You might object that detecting the deficit becomes obvious only after the election. It should be detectable in the voter registration rolls and in the algorithm of voter behavior in that state's districts. Since American society has been described as the most mobile in the world, with people changing jobs and residences quite often, it would not surprise anyone or cause concern to see people, in this case vetted and dedicated Democrat voters, relocate to a state where their vote is needed to cancel a voter deficit of the party in that state."

"Yes, this is an example of the numbers game of the strategy needed to put Hillary in the White House. I agree, if it had been used in 2016, she'd be president today. Since she isn't, having lost to Trump's campaign, which concentrated on winning in the Electoral College, her chance will come in 2020 if she chooses to run and can beat Bernie Sanders and Elizabeth Warren and whoever else in the Democrat party decides to seek the nomination. Hopefully that battle won't be as damaging or hard as her struggles in 2016. She had a very difficult time beating Bernie for the nomination, a 74-year-old Socialist from Vermont."

"I say the nomination is hers if she wants it. Apply this plan to her primary con- tests in key states, and she wins the nomination. The key is to put enough die-hard Democrat voters into the counties with a deficit to cancel out the deficit, adding a margin so winning is assured. She wins in such counties. Saturate the counties in key states that went for Trump in 2016, with just enough voters to swing them to Hillary. This is the winning strategy that will put her in the White House. If you can find a defect or flaw in it that makes it unworkable, please tell me what it is."

"The complaint has been that fighting the last battle won't ensure victory for the next one. While that in principle is true, neutralizing the Democrat vote deficit numbers of the last election in the next election at least does not indulge in the optimism that voting patterns will change back to favor Democrats in the Blue Wall states. We can't count on that electorate to come to their senses in time, so we need to plan to flood the zone with excess voters from states like California and New York, thus setting up the most likely outcome of a win for Hillary in 2020."

"In 2016, the 'safe states' of the Blue Wall states of Michigan, Pennsylvania and Wisconsin were where Trump beat Hillary. If he hadn't, she'd be president today. The consensus is she neglected them and did not campaign enough there or spend enough there. A political scientist might say she fell victim to asymmetrical mobilization. Of course not the kind of mobilization we're proposing here, but the old school type we are replacing with new thinking and a new approach to raw numbers and how to use them in a workable plan for victory. And we all agree deep in our guts that there is no substitute for victory, as we learned in the horrible pain of her 2016 loss."

"Trump did soundly defeat her in the states each side treated as the biggest battle- grounds – Florida, North Carolina, and Ohio. His breakthrough was in the Rustbelt states of the Great Lakes, Pennsylvania and Wisconsin. His winning margin was one percent or less. So you see we're not talking huge numbers of transplants needed in order to turn the races there for Hillary, if other factors hold constant."

"Can't the plan be used for Democrat Senate and House races? You bet it can, and lead to a majority again, in both chambers, like Obama enjoyed for the first two years of his first term, enabling him to pass the Affordable Care Act, his pet project. Nancy Pelosi knew no one had to read its thousands of pages, and she said so, and it passed without many reading it first. Not one Republican voted for it. That's the kind of ramming we can do again once this plan gets a Congressional majority again."

"An important variable is how Independent voters will go, not only in 2020, but in elections beyond, at both the state and national levels. How to factor this variable into calculating the numbers of transplants needed in any particular county and state? We can't let these elections, any of them, continue to be a crap shoot. We can't leave the outcomes to chance. We need to actively manipulate, legally and in compliance with all applicable laws, the numbers in our favor. That involves moving needed voters to where they do the most good, and not pile up excess votes in secure states while we lose in states that need only a relatively few transplants in order to win."

"Absolutely right. It's called rationalizing the process, allocating resources as needed, dedicated to accomplishing one goal, her winning the presidential election as the Democrat party candidate. 2020 has got to be her year."

"The party has been losing elections since 2010. Why hasn't that trend been turned around? Why does it take an outsider to come up with an idea that looks like it has a fool-proof strategy for winning and returning the party to majority rule?"

"The Pew Research Center says that overall, 35% of white registered voters identify as Independent, while about as many as 36% identify as Republicans, and fewer that 26% identify as Democrat. Overall, 48% of all registered voters identify as Democrat or lean that way, compared to 44% who identify as Republican or lean toward the GOP. Wide gaps exist among demographic groups. There are fundamental differences in how men and women, young and old, white, black, and Hispanics describe their partisan leanings. Persistent differences have grown wider in recent years."

"The party must not fail to distinguish its future from its past. It must transform its tired ideology and Bolshevik fervor into a post-partisan view of society, and get on board the mindset of a plugged-in, horizontal world of networks and autonomous value. It must abandon the hierarchy of power and enable, even empower individuals to realize their potential outside the prison of dependency. When they say 'party of the people,' what do they mean?"

"I think that proves the likelihood of our fondest dream coming true, that we could put anyone up as the party's candidate and they'd win. In early March 2017 Oprah said she saw no reason not to run herself. And Senator Al Franken, the ex-comedian from Minnesota, is setting himself up for a run. His setting up then Senator Jeff Sessions with a bait-and-switch question about talking to the Russian ambassador actually caused Attorney General Sessions to recuse himself from any probe into the matter by a special prosecutor. Those are the kind of political points Franken needs to create an image of credibility for himself. He hasn't got one yet."

"Right, and don't put it beyond the sports team owner Mark Cuban to run also. He wore a sweatshirt to a game in early March with the number 46 on it, as in president number 46 … get it? So the field is wide open for 2020 or 2024 and beyond. With our transplant strategy, any of those possibilities, and many others, as long as they can win the primaries and get the party's nod, can win the White House."

"As long as the Republicans don't counter with a neutralizing strategy of their own that moves their transplants around in time to key counties in swing states to pull out a win. They could tactically use their own numbers to more than balance out our own in certain districts. A few dozen votes, believe it or not, could prove to be the difference between victory and defeat for the White House."

"That's why our effort has to be as quiet and confidential as possible, for as long as possible. We can catch the Republicans off guard if we're careful, and they can never catch up, no matter how many transplants of their own they try to rush in, they'll be too late. It's all in the quantity and the timing, and location."

"You're absolutely right. That's how crucial every transplant can be. We need to consider every single one of them as the difference between Hillary winning the presidency or losing it in 2020. And we have to protect our offices against hacking and penetration by spies and double-dealing agents. And leakers, and eavesdropping through planted bugs, as was done to Trump Tower election headquarters in September and October of 2016. Trump claimed in a tweet storm in the early morning of March 4th, 2017 that Obama had done it, but the rebuttal did not mention the DOJ or the FBI, although FBI Director Comey came out and said he knew nothing of such a warrant. Such a non-denial denial turns out to be a confirmation."

"A FISA warrant from the secret court was needed for the wiretap. This is what police states do, use intelligence agencies against political enemies. The reporter James Rosen got caught up in that when Obama went after him. And when Obama directed the IRS to deny Tea Party related groups tax-exempt status so they couldn't afford to pursue political activity. The American people will learn what the Deep State is, using intelligence agencies as political weapons, to smear and hamstring the new administration, in a silent coup."

"James Clapper, DNI from 2010 to 2017, told Meet the Press on March 5th, 2017 that he'd know if there were such a warrant, and he denied there was one. But he did not say there was no warrant for a wiretap on Trump associates in Trump Tower. Russian investors in some of Trump's assets could be the target of the warrant and wire- tap. One of Trump's sons had said Russian money was pouring in. This is partly why we need to keep pushing that Trump needs to release his tax returns angle. We need to see if he is vulnerable to Russian influence monetarily."

"Hillary carried 26 districts of Representatives who were against Trump's repeal and replace Obamacare health insurance plan, the American Health Care Act, and in the end, on March 24th, 2017, brought Paul Ryan;s effort to get it passed in the House to failure – Ryan withdrew the bill instead of having it go down in defeat. So if we can target the right districts across the country, especially in key states narrowly lost in 2016, we can turn the Trump train around, or at least derail it."

"What would the musical you mentioned look like? What did you call it?"

"I'd call it 'Hillary 2020, the Musical – How She Can Win.' It would outline the strategy we've talked about, of paying the relocation expenses of willing and loyal Democrat voters to precincts in key states she lost in 2016, like in the upper Midwest. Utilizing most of those millions of 'excess' votes she got in states like Oregon, Washington, California, and New York would cover the vote deficit in states that Trump surprisingly won, and ensure her winning this election.

"The story line would be the arc of the election itself, including a prologue of lessons learned in her 2008 run, and in 2016 against Trump. This narrative would contain the drama, the conflicts, personal relations, and love interests of clearly drawn characters."

"So it's basically a play, with music, and singing songs, and dancing. So we'd need sets and designers, a composer, musicians who'd record the soundtrack, and a song writer for the lyrics, and a choreographer, and costumes. My nephew's wife's sister, an actress on Broadway in more than one big hit, has at least some of the contacts we'll need to get started. She might even portray Ann.

Between each scene and each act a video is projected on a wall of Madonna on the day of the Woman's March in Washington yelling to the crowd 'I have thought an awful lot about blowing up the White House!'."

"I see **Act One** as recounting the painful after-effects of election night, the wailing and gnashing of teeth in a new Hell. And the protests in the streets and in cities around the world. The Resistance Movement forming out of the anguish and anger. Dialogue would be conversations we've had, parts put to music and in the form of lyrics. Ann Crawford's entrance and rise would be lyrically portrayed, her contributions described in parts of all three acts. Here too the resettlement plan is introduced as a revolutionary way way to guarantee victory. Mostly by single, young people, and many on a temporary basis, who move to the target states in time to register to vote.

"In **Act Two**, more of our prior conversations are used as dialogue, parts put into song. Implementing the plan proves more difficult and complicated than first thought, but since it's a sound strategy, faith in it is re-enforced as statistical models keep churning out the right results. The hard work of recruiting voters willing to relocate adds drama to the story as the empathetic characters devote themselves to a massive task, one built on a dream and their fervent hopes for a woman they love and respect.

"Although carefully screened, some relocation candidates aren't as dependable as first thought. The skulduggery, double-dealings, and betrayals become all too frequent, almost as if applicants had been guided to the DNC selecting group. Volunteers who in fact did not have the party's or Hillary's best interests at heart. That's why connecting with committed true believers who sincerely want Hillary to get elected, who can be truly trusted, will make all the difference.

In **Act Three**, more of our prior conversations are used as dialogue, parts put to music in song and dance. In 2018 the Democrats lose even more seats to the Republicans, creating more anguish among the faithful hoping to get Hillary elected. As 2020 approaches, monitors detect Republican attempts to respond to our plan, but they're too late, they can't effectively counter the dominant numbers of our voters. She wins in the way anticipated by the plan, and rejoicing can be heard from coast to coast. Foreign capitals are also relieved Trump will no longer be at the helm. They welcome Hillary with open arms. It's a new day in America. Sighs of deep relief, and dancing in the streets. The future looks brighter."

3. <u>Title</u>: LEGAL IVORY – SAVING THE ELEPHANTS

<u>Genre</u>: Adventure, Political Intrigue, and Animal Conservation

<u>Logline</u>: Elephant lovers struggle to save them from ivory poachers by co-opting them into preservation efforts through financial and legal system incentives.

<u>Pitch</u>: By convincing certain African nations to provide adequate and appropriate incentives to ivory poachers, that is, convince them to wait until elephants die a natural death, and then to harvest their tusks for the ivory trade and demand in China for the supposed aphrodisiac properties, the elephant population can be saved from extinction.

<u>Description</u>: Story and documentary action to be developed on-site in sub-Saharan Africa, like other safari-adventure films have been made.

4. <u>Title</u>: LAHMU DENIED (MARS REBUKE)

<u>Genre</u>: Sci-Fi thriller

<u>Log Line</u>: Three-nation race to Mars turns out badly for two of them.

<u>Pitch</u>: Space program rivalry among Russia, China, and the US to get to Mars first. Treaty agreement prior to launches though has them arrive at the same time, but with different agendas and outcomes after they get on the surface.

<u>Synopsis</u>: Russia, China, and the US separately send astronauts in three separate craft on a recon mission to Mars, as a first stage in their planned colonization effort. Each craft is scheduled to land in the Cydonia region, and in the "The City" (photo-graphed from Mars orbit by NASA in the summer of 1976, a complex of huge, artificial structures, near to which are others, including a large pyramid, a long wall, a mile-long Face, and other objects that will need identification after landing).

Preparation for pre-flight is depicted at each nation's simulation facility – routines and procedures are practiced, with various problem-solving, emergency scenarios and solutions worked out with the support staff.
The home life and family of each country's astronauts are portrayed (like in the movie *Apollo 13*).
Preparation for launch, and launch and flight of each craft are shown, revealing more of the courage and grit of each crew member, and their close friendships.
As they approach Mars orbital insert, the Chinese craft shoots a long-range, satellite-killing laser at both the Russian and US craft, damaging them, partially disabling some systems on both.

Unarmed, they are unable to respond in kind, and barely manage to control their craft for de-orbital descent. They miss their planned landing sites by two and three kilometers respectively.

The Chinese alter their announced choice of landing site to near the "D&M Pyramid," determined to survey it and try to gain entry, based on their understanding of some Egyptian pyramid secrets divulged by researchers such as Bauval and Sitchin – power systems and energy sources built into their designs.

With damage to their craft and injuries to some crew members, the Russian and US crews struggle to minimize the setbacks, and devise ways to recover sufficiently to perform up to about 75% of mission specs. Parameters for mission completion are almost nominal. Repairs will take time away from surface exploration and documentation, but use of fuel and supplies previously sent to Mars for the return to Earth is feasible once the pre-positioned excursion vehicles are located and used for mission tasks.

The Russians and US radio each other to coordinate their plans, agreeing that the Chinese laser attack amounted to an act of war, and that they must be neutralized and stopped from accomplishing whatever it is they hope to do on Mars. They arrange a rendezvous of two armed team members from both crews, who meet and plan to attack the Chinese at their prescribed landing site.

They trudge to the pre-positioned supply base where all-terrain vehicles are waiting. From there they travel to where the Chinese are supposed to be, the south end of the mile-long "Face," but they're not there, and nowhere to be seen. They launch a drone in search of the Chinese craft and team, locating them near the NE corner of the "D&M Pyramid."

They plan and prepare for the attack, and execute it to good effect, destroying the Chinese landing craft and back-up systems, eliminating two of the four crew members, leaving the other two stranded, to fend for themselves.

The Russian and US teams, four members each, now realize their survival depends on cooperation and mutual support. Open conflict, from their natural rivalry, would not serve either of their mission goals, so for the moment they put Earth-bound conflicts aside and are determined to use cooperation as a means to survive.

The Russian cosmonauts have fatal accidents and make deadly mistakes that take them out of the competition to colonize Mars, setting their program back decades. The US team of four, made up of two men and two women, struggle to barely survive at first, then progress as they learn new coping skills.

They finally get to survey and map the Cydonia region, with its magnificent ancient structures, measuring and probing them as true explorers. They notice various mathematical relationships among the huge monuments that are so carefully laid out. Different mathematical constants, such as e over pi, are detected by the crew as they analyze the architectural data. They conclude that whoever designed and constructed them represented a magnificent and advanced civilization.

The only one that filled the bill, according to a scholar, Z. Sitchin, whom they had studied, was that the makers came from planet Nibiru, tenth planet of the solar system, known by the ancient Sumerians on Earth. Those from Nibiru first colonized in what is now southern Iraq. The Sumerians told the story of being taught, led and ruled by those from Nibiru, the Anunnaki

("From Heaven Those Who Came Down to Earth"). The ancients called Nibiru "Heaven" (*An*), and Sumerian for 'Earth' was *ki*.

Such conclusions would need to be put in their final report to NASA. What the officials did with the information could depend on the political climate at the time, and the public's state of readiness to hear such other-worldly conclusions, and the potential for contact if and when the makers of Cydonia might decide to return. But the evidence NASA had claimed it was looking for all these decades, in their search for extraterrestrial life, was now in their hands. What would they do with it?

5. <u>Title</u>: THE LIFE OF COINS

<u>Genre</u>: animated children's film

<u>Log Line</u>: coins and their adventures illustrated for children

<u>Pitch</u>: Each denomination of coin is depicted according to its reputation, personality, meme, and place in the kingdom of coins. Adapted to various countries' monetary system, different versions of this film have wide international potential appeal to youngsters around the world.

<u>Synopsis</u>: Each change coin tells its story, from creation in a forge to its travels to distribution center, bank vault, to the first person who put it in his/her pocket, purse or coin holder … to travels as it is passed from person to person in purchase transactions, even spending long periods of time in the dark of a piggy bank, in a bowl, in a drawer, lost on the floor, misplaced behind a couch cushion, and under a car's floor mat.

Each coin denomination has its own character, traits, personality, idiosyncrasies, habits, prejudices, beliefs, fears, hopes, likes and dislikes, and dreams.

The penny likes to pinch the other coins. The nickel prefers to plug any hole it finds. The dime prefers to stay as thin as possible and is on a perpetual diet.

The quarter can't help but divide everything it comes into contact with into whole fourths. The half-dollar has a compulsion to separate everything into two parts, and sees the world as divided against itself, as in one half against the other, and is always looking for its other, lost half.

[note to readers: some of these script treatment properties could be, by publication date of this book, under consideration by different producers, directors, and various agencies, in an assortment of development stages]

BOOK 2

COLLECTED POEMS, 1968-2017

(some published in 5 countries, and with at least one Nobel Prize winner for literature, Pablo Neruda, the Chilean poet, in *The Paris Review*, Winter 1971, 3 poems)

Special thanks to Saul Bellow (Literature Nobel Prize winner in 1976) for encouraging a young American writer living and struggling in Paris, France in 1966. His kind words in a personal letter sustained me for years.

In *Evergreen*, New York, Feb. 1968: an anti-Vietnam war poem. In edition with the famous cover portrait of Che Guevara:

Paris VC

All white races will be eaten
In Asia

The Viet Cong had rigged
Every dog and cat to die
At a person's touch

Americans are known
As death

I walk the streets of Paris and live
In the jungles of Vietnam
I slaughter and am slaughtered

In *Breakthru*, London, England, May 1968:

Bells of Birth

The bells of birth reverberate
Love through the ancient cosmos

Rose to its rest,
Its level beyond
Overwintering

Cruelly uneven
The windswept, scooped-out moon
Ever grates its ageless domain
Remains windless

In *Breakthru*, London, England, September 1968

It Is More

It is more
You are initiated
To many bronze
       in the long mud

I give you surface
To reaffirm the bread
Thousands of years of marble
Diminish the equation

In *Beyond Baroque*, Venice, California, August 1970:

Poem

Deathtrains will haul everyone away
on soft shoes
obliterate the 59th star, all 59 stars
and in soft clothes

A red car and a white girl
will get one with the other
is all I want

Steve Canada

In *Hearse*, Eureka, California, 1971

The Land is Good

The land is good

Holidays

Marry Xmas,
Happy Easter,
Bon Voyage, etc.

In *The Paris Review*, Winter 1971, three poems:

Rain

In bars of cement light
Orange suns chain across the sky

After the consuming rain
Blistered our mouths
Leaves fell and laid on one another

Bird

A heavy bird in flight ripples
To baby crystals, baby birds
Fly through the thick light

I listen to the window be
Cause you can see through it

Poem

Did you see blood
on his shoulder,
Strange dust?

The ancient customs of a gracious people

In *The Paris Review*, Fall, 1972, two poems:

Black Sea Girls

Passing through,
passing through the sea's afternoons

Empty of robin's eggs
we walk through the thick lizard

Black Sea girls
bump and grind, rock and roll

We Believe Like Wildfire

We believe like wildfire
In a hair-like echo

Silences of darkness are
Windows into water

Windows Into Water, poetry collection booklet published by Chiva Publications, Boulder Creek, California, October, 1973: (excluding previously published poems, as reproduced here) –

Love's Map

On the earth run wild with seed
you wash me
Laughing … lying on you
my fingers no nearer than the bone
You sleep in both my hands
This, inaudible, prefers the sap of the lips
In the morning of high fire
I grasp your full breasts and
you rock me to the tune of my dying

Children Kissing in the Bathroom

In the arms of the sun
we wait for guns aimed at
the brown and the black
A conspiracy to kill the children
more interested in kissing in the
bathroom than digging a grave with
their left hands

Breathe My

I breathe my father
built upon the earth's
free and easy music
The color of what
bird after bird is
to the fruit
In the deadwood sky,
why the tongue breaks
bones even though it has none

Father Brimstone Dancing

over the brim of the people running
you had no lips when I first saw you

every moment together brimstone
dancing/ chirping through the
hollow sky

Steve Canada

Poem to John Berryman, Poet

Didn't you learn John that
life goes on?
John, life goes on.
Jesus Christ, that
water must have been cold!

When they fished you out of
that river, whoever they were,
did they know who they had hooked?
Did they know your dreams, your songs,
your seventy-seven lives?

When they gaffed you to
shore like a whale of
a poet you were, every
bug on every branch must
have bowed once in
honor of your passing.

Your drowning, your blubbering for breath,
when death froze your
legs, stretched your arms out
on the cross of the
bridge you crossed, the
bridge you didn't cross.

The Poison Season

In the poison season of the wild ponies
ugly jelly marbles follow the
village's button sickness, its
awful powers.

Arrows and letters are traded.

Learning to Eat Time

A certain glass pride
touches the silence
so vast you cannot hear it

The first men and the last
must learn to eat time,
journey into stone with the
hunter's moon

Signed in the Stone

Silver sea planes seek
the secret of winged bones
As I watch giant birds gouge
flesh from the sea

Signed in the stone
rain falls and
wounds my nursing mouth

Metal Eagles

Organic tapestries hang in
metal clumps, kite hair

The eagles that Hitler launched

Only the passion that they were,
only the fashion that they were

Parties of bottoms capture the circle of
circus perfume picnic,
pictures in the summer.

Certain things are added: tennis cucumbers,
other things are subtracted: badminton
asparagus,
multiplied: ping pong artichokes,
and divided: basketball avocados.

The Death of Animal Music

A healthy death's fiery flute plays
catch with the high-flying plane.
It swoops down to sing the
screaming mountain to sleep.

A rolling ball of beans
reads the car back onto the road,
around a deer and home through
an avalanche of unique touchings.

You were not there to listen
so the storm is rising
even stronger than it had been
tempted by you.

A fat, rafter possum,
using a tulip as its rudder, and
singing alto cantata fortissimo,
translates the grammar of the rising river.

Poem

this poem is the way a life breaks
the silence of a night cracking
around itself to hold a heart that

cannot jump from its mole hole
I forced the world through the hoop
and it is here now, in front of you

Mountain Way

He put his fingers into and
through ripe crystal

Stones across the valley, hum

Lizard Tongue

It keeps going in and out and
has no answers

I take back my lizard tongue

Yes, there is a bird, even a lizard
and my tongue, with their tongues
when all spoke the same language,
when all mated with the same cry

nuts the shape of water drops

Float through the spider air
along the mountain way

Float along the blue and
pink opaque rim of the world

In *Espresso*, Number 1, 1973, Pacifica, California (3 small poems):

Three Line	**Poem Name**	**Poem**
(blank line)	a name,	the side that is green on
poem	any name	(sing as lullaby three times,
(blank line)		vary color)

In *The Carleton Miscellany*, Fall/Winter 1973-74, Vol. XIV, No.1; Carleton College, Northfield, Minnesota:

Birds Fly in and Out of Her Body

(for Carole, my then wife, whose support and
encouragement made my creative work possible,
including paintings shown in juried shows all over
southern California, 1969-72)

She knows
the terror inside her mouth

Fears her flesh
the love in her

Birds fly in and out of her body

In *Canto*, Swoyersville, Penn., December 1973:

Her Popcorn Mouth

I kissed her popcorn mouth
denying between hers lips
the world had a flat belly

lizard feathers

hard, dry water,
a sculpture of the wind

In *Eureka*, Stockholm, Sweden, May 1974, 3 poems,
not reproduced here, but titled: 'Fidel,' "Che,' and
'Pablo and Allende.'

In *Northern Light*, number 1, Winter 1974; University of Manitoba, Winnipeg,
Canada, R3T 2N2:

Handfuls of Lips

As we swoosh down the avenue
arm-in-arm to the penny arcade
we ride the waning moon high and home.

In the morning her lips know,
they understand completely.
She speaks directly to the body.

The grey hand of dawn
strikes from our teeth
some unseen name.

In one fell swoop of her hips
her tangerine sighs make me sing

A great apricot fire softly
encircles our sleep.

The bright image of her face still
shines in the dumb darkness.

Steve Canada

We search for and find
each others name in the rain.

In the wild waters where we love
her slightly arched arms show
perfect *porte de bras*.

Our voices, raised together under a
scooped-out moon,
show us how to read the water.

In her island heart I caress
the spontaneous celebration of euphoria.

We search through the sea for that moment,
our birthday place in time.

Heart-high in the wallowing waves
we emerge from the surf a member of
the ultimate nation of cleaving couples.

Our desire for each other rings like
Japanese wind chimes through dense pines.

Infinitesimal yellow flowers
blossom in our flesh.

Large white birds fly
great arcs in the scarred sky.

Dawn breaks tingling in the winter morning.
Storming birds rape the frost for seed.

She lays open to me in her small room,
giving birth to something clear and whole.

exploding on the tips of my fingers
into the vast, sensuous subtleties of summer.

We travel together a high mountain road.
Hop scotch truth skips through our
fairyland enigma, this grapefruit landscape.

Handfuls of lips come to the nearby lake.
Legs entwined and hands singing

we lie in each others arms,
babbling in each others ear.

My sparkling breath in the swirling air
forms fragrant stones.

The ineffable lyricism of our bodies
undulates in our thick human movement.

A huge heart circles us with vast visions of
what can be done and what can be undone.

Running nude in the cavernous rain,
lost among the trees' messages of rocks

she hears landscape voices, hooves in
deep snow, great birds breaking the earth.

Swimming in fires of the river
we bathe in the hot thick breath of the soil
the gentle moss forest against our mouths.

In her finger-deep fur I am
wrapped in her youthful joy, in her sadness.

Her voice is the skin of magic,
covers the moments around her with
nuggets of cryptic grace.

She sustains a spell that invites me
to dissolve into glowing silver,
lips rising on the wind.

In *Eureka*, Stockholm, Sweden, Winter 1975-76: 5 poems –

Fire Fast

In the thick dark air
fire fast consumes the
nothing that is left.

The whole earth is
flames as the looming moon bulges
into the heavy abyss of
this humid, diaphanous night.

Down the horizon
fish climb into the sky.
The sky is where I understand the desert,
know what it is to fear the moon,
to eat anything that moves,
drink against a silhouetted sky.

She Speaks Whole Water Chestnuts

She speaks whole water chestnuts.
The Northern Lights go out when
her train whistle blows.
Dogs bark and the stillness gets darker and
darker and darker.

She has surfaced from her romance.
All the world drowns in her sorrow, in the
flood of her violet mouth, her orange
juice heart.

The air shines with a great white slime.
Shadows perfume the jeweled light.
Aligned to form the shore, stones
upon the bent sea.

A certain glass pride touches the silence so
vast you cannot hear it.
The first men and the last must learn to eat time,
journey into stone with the hunter's moon.

Rag birds pearl the dense night,
fly in the body of all flying things.

Spring birds in Winter water
hear the thick sun –
drunk with bunched eyes,
in a slow mood of Mediterranean slippers –
put them in its jewelry box.

"Le Paradise de Orages S'effondre"
(A. Rimbaud, *Illuminations*)

The rape of the Messiah in her
unbreakable pain –
her eggs of worms are laid with
the larva of the living in the
tombs and tongues of time
where they fall prey to the beast.

She is all eyes and hair.
"This paradise of storm collapses,"
flies in the teeth.

The long march of the lizard under
a true pale blue sky, one now deep
in the mind of the aborigine who
hears the footsteps and
believes he is the dreamed,
deep enough to walk through the ancient fire,
take the planet's air.

Primordial words lie on the ground with
dead tongues eating
the words know to all men.
Hawks' eggs under a scooped-out moon are
marinated by the darkness.

A ghost of a lime-green sunset eaten
with bare hands, eaten with the fire that
boils our senses and scatters them to the wind
joins the fear of desire and shapes the grunt
and gruff of visible, exclaimable urges.

The Poet's Prerogative

The fading perfume of our bodies
mingles in the grave of other men.
With you I hear my own drinking as
the tide rises to the lips, and higher.
My fear that is already extinct dies
before you are undressed.

Do you fake everything or am I destroying
what there is left to hope for by
parading in front of you, by working up a
sweat, by saying I take that seriously, by
making a fool of myself, forgetting what you are?
Your perfect mouth sings to my soft body,
breaks my eyes, pours the salt of the past
into the wound of the present.

It's the poet's prerogative and pain to
fall in love. You and I
have already killed each other, made the other
unreal through money, the god almighty
dollar. But that will not stop me from
dragging around a cherished image.
Je veux que ce coeur durci ne traine plus
une chere image.

In the migration that pours honey over my life
I drive right through rock, over spines of snow.
I've waited for you, hung out for you like an outlaw.
My own innocent depravity fuses with your
whore's heart and we make the perfect couple.

Our future is pretending it is here,
after and before the fact of what fantasies
remain undone.I live beyond the means of
moment, beyond what I know cannot come,
beyond what must be done, the only way to
cover the miles, the only way to see
ice across your eyes – get close with a
black pimp's knife and see how it cuts.

Yet there is more – you standing vulnerable,
resentful in the circle of slaves,
guarding your integrity with a ferocious
willingness to be used … proving to everyone
you cannot be touched.

I only ask you to come as you are so we
can burn together and sail into those silky
moments, our time in your small room as long
as the beginning, as large as the next instant

when our laughter eats the universe, milks the stars.

In *Poetry Scope*, Menasha, Wisconsin, March 1982:

Shadow Daughter
(for Tracy)

At dusk she remains where I cannot
reach her, my shadow daughter.
After the time of shiny noses powdered with marshmallows
the rendered heart, wondering, eats ice cream.
She says she is the daughter of subsequence and consequence.
She is a child of hot chocolate, the constant, cruel
generations between our voices
no bar to our hands holding, our
eyes each other touching.

The sandcastle day laden with adult hope
I choose and
finger clothes for her, fit them to her imaginary form,
estimate with movements of my mouth
monuments that imprison the heart (errant knight
happy prisoner of the Sea Queen)
their own fearful lightness singing to a
future in need of a past.
Alone at the foggy sea, she dances in the surf.
With patience we will reap the courage to
walk into the natural light of who she is,
who I am and who we are togther.

The following poems are some I wrote when I lived in Milwaukee, Wisconsin for a year, through June, 1986. They were collected into a small booklet, *The Milwaukee Poems*, in 1986, and are dedicated to Lisa, my girlfriend at the time. I read most of them during a radio interview at the University of Wisconsin, Milwaukee in May, 1986. "I Feed on Her Like a Winter Bird" appeared in the *Wisconsin Review*, 20th anniversary issue, UW, Oshkosh, May, 1986. "Poem,' the first poem below, was published in an international anthology, *World Poetry*, (570 pages, Sacramento, Calif.,1986). Several of the other poems collected for the volume appeared in *Goethe's Notes*, Milwaukee, edited by Jesse Glass, in 1986 and 1987. Thanks to Bilhenry Walker, sculptor, who made Milwaukee possible for me, a place of spiritual rejuvenation, magic and love, and intense poetic engagement.

Steve Canada

Poem

My eye words fly right off the
lip of the heart.
Deeper than her hair is black my
hungry caring fears for her sadness.

Breathing her skin my hands speak a new language.
Touching the magic of her
desire leaps up like a fish out of the river,
into the water of our lives mingling with
the sea yet to come.

The core of belief entwines in her --
I merge with nature through her,
god flowing everywhere.

The way she holds herself against me, slowly moves
her head back, opens her mouth in complete receptivity,
arches her back, lets her head fall all the way back,
her hair touching the ground –
her silent expression of faith in our desire, a
letting go, so our feelings can fly free.

"They Keep Coming Back to the River"

We stand and hold each other on the river's bank.
The way she falls back I catch her, fall into her.
Her full lips stop in mid kiss, her
passive feminine slowness opens my
heart with the crowbar of need.

She jumps up on me, wraps her legs around me.
After our separate winters we bath are
exploding in this Milwaukee spring.
Near Juneau bridge, at our harp music dinner, she said
"They keep coming back to the river."

We went back to the river for love.
We laid there Indians 10,000 years ago.
Ancient thunder, ageless lightning spoke for our
unready bodies, "too soon" the tune of the river's song.
Nature's kind storm chased us through the parched fields,
the rain baptizing our overeager skins.

After getting lost, first in her long dark hair, then
further lost again in her dark brown eyes
I asked her "Now what am I going to do?"
She always says "I don't know."
She touched me, she touched my photo at twelve,
touched the boy inside me.

Milwaukee

I arrived in the city in the night,
I will depart this magical place in the night,
yet the light shone all in
my hundred days here.

My sojourn to this meeting of the rivers,
my journey among the lighted faces, my
travels through these intricate hearts, graced with
a Milwaukee love that blesses this Milwaukee air.

We keep coming back to the river.
We stand in the water, join ourselves in its flowing.
In our four-way flowing we learn the language of all
rivers, of all water, of all lovers.

After our theater of my adoration she told me
"I had fun too, I enjoyed sculpting the wind."
The air itself holy, paradise flying off her in the
star-thin light, clouds again
move above her still visage.

She Spreads Paradise

Making love on the half moon we
learn on the cusp of the river's true tongue.

We do simple, natural things together.
In her torn tee-shirt she sculpts the wind,
sits in my lap, leans far back, spreads
her flying arms.

We can't help but stop time, the
middle of the night held at bay
'til it surprises us.

We kiss with the slowest lips this great
lake has ever witnessed.

We love in the river's plants – thick and
grey-green under our half moon – they
touch us as we move into each other

With the knowledge of all that is gentle, all
that is wild in the water, we
gurgle with new voices as the earth
pushes us in rhythm to its body,
our one body two faces joined at the heart

We will love standing in the river,
both nude to our half moon.

She carries paradise with her,
spreads it around wherever she stays.
It comes off her skin, the way she moves,
her smile its cause.

Moments in the Eyes

Linked by the cawing of crows
by the river we stand
in ways no man or woman before have stood.

Our twelve senses merge.
She mediates totality. She does this by
herself, alone.

I am only witness, coupled through desire.
She shapes the air, sheens the light,
gurgles the water.

There are moments in the eyes,
my left hand on her right hip
who know the meaning of oneness,

Who know what it is to be holy
in all seasons blessed with Grace on the
last, fullest moon.

We Sleep Like Indians

I speak to the stars over and over again,
one to each – "I love Lisa," "I love her."

In the dark silence the
galaxy's bell reverberates.

Her heart shines – in the
vastness of space she holds me.

Cheetahs chase us through the jungle.
We sleep like Indians next to the river.

We peer into each other like the
moon peers into stone.

We pieces each other like water
seeps into the earth.

I Feed on Her Like a Winter Bird

I wear clothes older than she is.
The snow keeps falling.
She shovels the sidewalk.

She keeps moving me in and out of her life.
She keeps moving me.

I feed on her like a winter bird.
The naked trees have abandoned their
luxury of leaves.

I must close off the sap in
order to survive.

The Swans of Mequon

I have seen the swans of Mequon.
I have walked the marsh alone.
I remember that November – she
came to me, returned to me again –

linked by he cawing of crows my
totem crows winging their way around us.

I missed her in the night, committed my
self to her by traveling up, through the
Great Spirit's crystal mandala on
swan's wings, on her spread arms sculpting the
magical spring Milwaukee wind.

On the green brush around the pond where
our arctic swans rest on their southward flight
the soft crush of our tramping feet
will remember that one November Sunday
when we were all-in-one day.

It's Lisa or no one.
It's the swans of Mequon or no migrating birds at all.
She cannot be a girl I once knew.
They cannot be swans I once saw.
We could follow them, these wandering beauties.
We could be together every day, on the wide white wing,
on the wide warm wind.

Disturbing the Interstellar Hydrogen

The stars hear me, they will hear my oath, my
faith, my screaming need of her.
She wore her torn tee-shirt, slept with me,
didn't call me for three days,
She knew what she was doing. She's done it before
confession. She Doesn't know how to talk to me.
She knows how to go to the center, shred it, walk away.

Out loud I told the December stars.
One by one they saw my lips move,
one by one they shone steady, one by one they were silent.

I gave the cold night my voice – to the
edge of the deep atmosphere it floated, one
repeated "I love Lisa, I love Moo Moo" behind
the other, bumping the thin, scattered gases
beyond the earth, disturbing the
interstellar hydrogen, sending my message to

all the stars, to all the lights, to all the
places in all the universe.

Saturday Night Vigil Confirmed

The only sensible thing to do is to move 2200 miles east to
be near a 20-year-old girl who sometimes wants me.
The best Saturday night this poet ever spent was outside a
teenage girl's house, on vigil for any sign of her.

That night was the last night of her nineteenth year.
The next day I was in a Catholic cathedral watching her take
confirmation. She saw me as she walked out with her
three friends. I stared at her. She smiled. My legs shook.
I knew she was for me.

She went down on her knees to receive the holy mark.
I went down on my knees to her at our river where we
received union, the holy river blessing us.
Marked by what I knew would destroy me I kept
living days to the fullest.

I carry the stigma of my stare, her eyes burrow into me.
I carry her face with me, a possessed visage. She knows
who she wants to marry, she knows how to walk on water,
she knows how to drown me.

The next section of poems below were written mostly while living on the island of Nahant, off the
Northshore, north of Boston, Mass., in 1987. Thanks to Paul Fiore, a long-time friend, for making
living in Nahant (an 'island' joined to Lynn by a cause- way) possible; a very special, peaceful
place by the sea, a place where writing become for me again a natural part of my life – a full year
of respite and recovery after my year in Milwaukee, Wisconsin (a place of spiritual transformation,
love and intense poetic inspiration).

Nahant

The night tortures me, the day tortures me.
The morning asks me questions, the evening gives me answers.
The afternoon sleeps with me, teaches me that dreams shine
on the water I am learning the patience and peace of this place.

Divide the Heart

Divide the heart into parts, add the heart into wholes,
multiply the heart into pieces, subtract the heart into bits.

Left is an equation that balances the air thick with memory,
images of her presence. The calculus of our mutual synergy
is our wings flapping.

Life is for only so long. We both knew it. That's why we
touched each other. It added up to more than we
knew was coming.

The Island

Our last day of loving became
the day of last loving. We have
one more cemetery to explore together.

Fragments of Eden in the garden of the gods lie
scattered on the island that began with misery became
the island of more than rhapsody, more than
touching what was left of eternity.

Like the never-ending snake and the
alone winging crow, together we heard
over the widening water
the hand-carried music of goodbye.

Grace

Down river I hear you
calling upwind we no longer swim
beside each other's angel.
I stand my ground and stay calm.

We explore the state of grace, become
its naturalized citizens.

A thousand miles is nothing between us.
I hail the palpable memory of you whole.
I whisper your name to my cat.
The air is sweet.

Island Promise
   (for Teri)

Joined in "please'
and the wine
mouth to mouth

In the park
against the railing
hands and bodies one
great river of love

Alone in the loft
his voice
out of my throat

In the dune grass
a promise to swim
the length of the lake

Love her he said
and I promised,
kept the promise
we island gods

The Price of Many Dreams
   (for Teri)

My hormones insist on getting all
dressed up for it.
Kissing like crazy
I feel the river pulling you
closer to me.
The water flows in awe.

Converts to passion, we
dance in the light surrounded by the
unrelenting island night

distance greater than the heart can hold,
greater than we were ever close,
the distance a death is carried,
the distance we both die.

Steve Canada

Her Gaze of Thunder

(for Teri; in *Goethe's Notes*,
Milwaukee, Summer 1986)

like a wounded rock
a man aligns his blood with
the earth

he sees her, touches her
    and knows

her "inner ear" is his
"in her hear," …
her gaze of thunder

we play the earth's music,
all of it a promise

Her Eyes of All Eyes

(for Teri; in *Goethe's Notes*,
Milwaukee, Summer, 1986)

I told her everything is free,
hire myself out to destiny,
free-fall to her the full length of
all the light there can ever be.

The vortex my dancing partner,
her always present,
our two hearts shot through with
each others blood.

Our only reason to be together is to
make no promises.
On the razor edge of minutes we decide
what can be and what cannot be.

The Right Woman

I knew the right woman would find me.
I knew the right woman would say no.

The right woman found me,
stood there on the deck, promised to call.

The right woman said yes-no,
brought me to see everywhere
the face of god.

Blue and Green

I live my days like a gumball machine.
I kick m/y/our self in the Humpty Dumpty.

The colors French blue and forest green will
save my life.
I sit in the dark and say to m/y/our self: 'Paint."

I live just beyond the east ocean,
just beyond the front of (y)our eyes,

... her yes eyes,
her yes mouth.

Unkept Gardens

Unkept gardens do not forgive the
unplanted seed that cannot grow.

We are keepers of this place,
ringers of the bells,
one-way mating ... never undone

we eat together,
echo the wind chimes,
reflect the sunned sea.

It is enough now to
feed wild winter birds and
close my eyes to spring light.

Steve Canada

Dawn

Her crayons melted in St. Louis.
We agreed that it was in Georgia.
She asked me for a ride. I drover here there.
I took her picture.
She kept smiling at me.
I cannot say No to her.
She asked me for ten dollars.
I gave her my only, crisp one.
She told me what the most
popular three lies are.
Our photo together proves something.
When she move to Cleveland
there will be no more summer.

Lobstering Morning, Nahant

A brave trio, our small band of
lobstering sailors, drank in
the dawn together.

Doing the ancient work of the sea,
we kept our sea legs on the
smooth water.

Diane chugged along better than
we could guide her, knew her way
among rocks hidden under the high water.

Our balance among each other,
taken on cue from the Egg Rock birds,
became what used to be a way of life.

New traps in and old traps up,
always the engine, hands working the
ropes, tying where and when to the food.

Blood on the bait. The wheeling birds and
that morning's sea air made me know:
the flight is all.

The following poem appeared in the Fall 1991 edition of *Coffeehouse Poets' Quar-terly: A Magazine of Contemporary Poetry*, San Luis Obispo, California, on p.31:

For All, For Always

evangelical night birds
persuade the Big Dipper to
wheel round the world
to sing the light
the light that takes … forever

in the palm of your loving hand
on the wing of a bird that knows its way
the cries of little children with
tongues in their mouths

in this moment I give you my eyes
y mi corazon tan bien
por todo, para siempre

The following 5 "dense text" poems were written in 2004;
there are hundreds more from that period, deserving of a
whole book of their own):

Tribal Refrigerator

a gingko biloba in my snapple is there for the power of the earth to
flow through you not command it with an out of balance
ego the difference between the power of self and eternity

standing in the shallow surf alone on a small beach letting the
waves do tai chi with you as the larger sea plays all the
appropriate ratios of music stunned by an improbably dramatic verdi

the song irresistible to gearbox tested cinematic oval tracks
on the sabbath of the stop sign at the speed limit of
transcendent brewed coffee drunk on the altar of overflowing gutters

lost to a misguided motor made of diamonds devoid of the
mantle's tectonic bedrock as measure of what is enlightened by
the big dipper's red oleander wasted in the abused tribal refrigerator

Bouncing Ball

whomever can accomplish such a balance can
stay awake forever unfurled in the master clock

with arms like that the battle is engaged upon a
fitted jeweled ring around the rosey

out of clear oxygen on its own accord webcam
tracking of all the stationed soldiers

coming to address the terms of the text altered
news from a world cast beyond recognition

spark plugs sequenced to fire in order to
preserve the hidden moment from plain view

take baby steps toward the throbbing recliner something
atmospheric pressure alone could not accomplish

fifth dimensional fingers caught in secret sand-filled
elapsed time caught by the coffee-organized bouncing ball

Feeding Tube

admitting its speedometer into the stove-piped club
but used wisely and consecrated as futile while at
the same moment erased as skinny tommy-gun green rays

eel grass subcutaneous worldbeat prays for the pinochle of
autumn darkness its software none the wiser chirping in
the dried-out tree addressing the ability to say no more

an ultimatum backslides into a baritone belonging to a
depressed chimp in the zoo watching the clock quadrupled
by falling asleep near the babbling brook tinged with

brow-beaten ether the editor of all that there is looking over the
snowball-soft gonad expensive in its pinstriped epidermis
addresses the book listing all the terror-training madrases

in the land of the two holy places cared for and stood in
by unquestioning infidels paid in dollar-coping mechanisms
called food and hair falling out of the feeding tube

Avowed Dentistry

the neutron warhead giggling all the way to the bank-shot
walled off by coca cola can irradiated conclusively by any
handyman devoid of input hesitating to puppy-love
any carved magic image of Charlemagne on his perquisite horse

antitropic algebra crafts the frequency modulated equation at
the loose mercy of limits climbing a wall of stock market worry
conjugated for ablative nouns by objective cases of dabbling
verbs the subjunctive state denied each burial

as if they breathe under water balanced on the edge of
a final circle contemptuous cadenza peers more
attentively turning a bronchial eye to recycling
plastic liquids weeded by regimented easels

state of the art not a drudged boot-strapping sword of
a loser bridesmaid maximized by the Adriatic throwing the
erased crossing point at this place of booty bulldozer
mobster-concealed corruption slaves to officially avowed dentistry

Tabulated Axis

on the bowstring of honeydew immunity rouge runs down
wampum bounty in the nascent isosceles cheekbone
cresting in the inspired injured mouth sweaty as dead wood

glowing clacking asiatic sofas grown in buckskin
embryology initiated by forlorn bullseye handouts
gigantic typeface cartoons know the secret difference

on the seventieth train artifacts of a cynical ruckus
lacerate all remaining couplings dispersed in playroom
parlor cars bobbing along first-edition steel tracks

composed by Adam as a lanky excuse for poisoning
evening songs focused to elapse the despised drill-bit
robust in its therapy checking its divested trivia at the door

compelled opera triumphs cut off indentured jeopardy
calling mangled diet essays the sticky salons from
whence constant retention bridges the electro bellboy market

absent infiltration how do a dozen libraries dare anvil
cathode osmosis swung by greenhorn offerings varied along
the infrared spectrum culminating on the tabulated axis

Poem (from 2007)

swim in the trivia of an infrared twinkle standing
straight as your neediest aim is true count and apply her
taking it for granted as her fear you won't give it or to
anyone parked in the handicapped zone remember upended
compost put a motor around my fat neck and freeze dry my
blood tears on QVC with diamond heart rings of angels
five solving the ethereal hydraulics of time of earned
understanding navigating grace through
musical notes guided by individual degrees of
kindness kissing ass and taking names while
glorifying in his canary-yellow urine balanced as a
more alkaline metabolism ingests the bacteria needed to
survive any attack from any quarter

Poem (from 2007)

(inspired by Ingmar Bergman's 1957 film
Wild Strawberries; the scene of 'the professor's
strange dream')

only the heartbeat of time
no hands on wild strawberries walk
this way to the dream where
blood flows as an omen of an
interrupted end when caskets are
dislodged into the street and you
meet yourself in the casket until
Swedish light resurrects you

Poem (from 2008)

the finished aftermath of empty space stuck in a
time warp warding off the bride of lesbian cabbage
soup testifying against itself in the trial by the sea

walk in that whitest finest Carmel sand by yourself

because there is no rescue in female company there is
no penalty in the box office of tapioca perdition

butterscotch weight loss only scares away the rabbits
each in their turn turned to stone by drops of her Pepsi
obsessed to the point of enchantment I watch an army die

[poems from 2009-11 would go here]

Legal Foraging (poem from 2012)

legal foraging/ soap opera out of traffic/ there be yellow clouds
in the larger sleep/ the smallest divine arrow/ wind leaves shadow birds
anxiety germs/ a beat you can really hear/ that's why I found him
the devil's halo/ penetrates the static code/ get it while it's there
these arthritic toes/ my machete cuts through time/ ignorant of games
aligned with the stars/ seven seasonal triumphs/ of proper pairings
crows as my totem/ dance in the open sky/ speak my language
hide behind trash cans/ vegetables sown for free/ to lactating men
his mind of Islam/ pulling the trigger of love/ as Allah commands
bending of the bones/ pulse as the meter of hate/ faithful to teachings
voting paradox/ middle of the night hipness/ prays to the ATM

Those Wise-Ass Rainbows (poem from 2012)

those wise-ass rainbows/ enough of pastel colors/ saying what they mean
these elastic mouths/ afraid to break tradition/ speak kindly of time
with the right spices/ unite with the infinite/ eat Indian food
my artichoke heart/ my Sphinx cat watching tv/ the history goddess
forest fire smoke/ disappeared like lightning/ from the Big Dipper
will she forgive me/ my scream over the decades/ east-facing fire
yes, kiss the dreamer/ bubble gum psychic warfare/ we know the difference
linking eye to ear/ listen to one drop of rain/ rule the pajamas
slip into the sea/ asking no more rude questions/ sleeping with the wind
full spectrum chem trails/ destroying our religions/ saving the planet

Poem (from 2012)

the desires of a burglar
against the sound of the natural sky
ask only one question

trivial as a tone of death
encoded in the Torah
each name of war dead
known to the memory of all memory

undifferentiated in the mass of the
Higgs Boson discovered in a Swiss
bank vault doing cartwheels,
preparing for the London Olympics
knowing itself through the mass of
contrition divided from itself

Poem (from 2013)

time is a bacteria eating the universe at the
speed of dark

lending soup to strangers creates a debt
even forfeit can't erase

money stolen does not disappear, it
becomes owed by a brother who buys a wife
and musical instruments, feeding on a
fantasy of fame

clocks tear apart the world one tick tock
at a time, deconstructing the fabric of space
with ricocheting energy so tiny we can't
notice it

Poetry Reading (for 2013)

Poems with ringing of a gong bell between each.

Explain at end that "the poems were actually the
bell ringing, and the words were only to fill in
the spaces between, to distract the wandering
mind from the false path."

Poem (from 2015)

a uniform painted in another language
the muted remains of ethically folding your underwear
some questions never get answered
industrial television encroaches on my identity
prayers up in smoke on a Chinese clock

Poem (from 2016)

the scars of friendship
escape down the dumbwaiter

death tides are due at 1:30 pm
break the bounds of language

a foreign tongue in the heart
recognizes moments, one at a time

at the mercy of spices
unnecessarily delicious

in the kingdom of doubt
tango will bring tears to your eyes

Poem (from 2016)

ice cubes, like lost children
jump out of the fast food machine,
like they're escaping the
tyranny of friendly, tasty fat

tasty because the pacific Ocean has
more salt than the Atlantic, more
appeal in its deeper voice, its
deeper canyons gouged by a rogue planet

lopsided Eridu (Earth), home in the
faraway ffor returning Anachim of
Nibiru, biblical Olam of the last
judgment, Torah-encoded End of Days

Poem (from 2016)

giving shadows substance
the hunter's moon is best left alone
with what a cat can't resist
helpless against their music

marriage fromage on Friday smells
fishy / Gibraltar was not a forgery
one honeymoon night in Tangier
came to out European rescue

he makes wire horses / married
72 hours and his husband
died in the land of opportunity
he lives alone in a ghost town
with his deaf dog

Poem (from 2016)

I believed that kiss would
go on forever, the way she held it.

It took a thousand mile breakdown
to destroy me.

She looked like all the beautiful
music ever composed by unknown
mortal glass animals.

The next 2 poems were published in the February 2017 edition of *The PEN* (Pittsburgh, Penn.):

Koan Poem

twitch not the leg of fortitude,
question only thine forearm as a
weapon of despotic peace

and then forgive the kidney that
betrayed you to each friendly foot
long ago the deal of the century

eat each aching tooth fried with
tortured bacon between afternoon bread
devined as answers to non-questions

"On The Trail of Tears"

on the trail of tears
heart-broken Cherokee blood
known for forgiveness

a clear-eyed dragon
little bits of affection
all possible truths

toddlers learn so much
all fundamental forces
while including love

snowman as side-man
in a band of ice-sickles
writer's discontent

my secret cancer
whose slice into existence
comforts the masses

a snake on its side
in a universal yawn
daylight in its mouth

organized babies
like the leaves on the south wall
freaks of a future

Two more poems from 2017:

An Army of Sparrows

an army of sparrows
bewildered by a
transfusion of memory
known only to true dinosaurs

asking forgiveness from the pure of heart
those questions forgotten in the nick of time-
keeping in London while up north
short-changing the private school boys

upside down the Big Dipper ushers
Orion to the horizon as snow
geese snuggle in the winter park
dreaming of their spring flight north

Calibrate the Threat

in the pecking order of charm
flattering a cat might save your life

I need more and more neurological insights,
until the cosmos unwinds itself and opens its heart

that would conquer death and help the
gentlest gesture survive

put some lasagna on your feet,
use a handkerchief elbow in mixed company,
calibrate the threat

(and two more haikus, from 2017; I've
written hundreds of unpublished kaikus):

more a broken stone
violating its contract
with eternity

a quandry of quail
upon the neglected tree
her load-bearing lungs

Two Alien Language Poems (translated):
An Interplanetary Literary Aesthetic
(in an unknown year; time was suspended;
and I've written other 'alien language' poems,
in different 'alien languages;' I could collect

enough for a whole book, if any publisher
is interested) – –

Nothing But the World

She can reach only so far singing
throat pointing to her left and
dancing for all the people to know her

    (Nothing But the World
She can reach only so far singing with
her throat pointing to her left
dancing for all the people to know her)

Burying the Future

Burying the future in works of the bench
restarted cueball trick shots at truck stops
tear uplink motoring every discarded mouth

    (Burying the Future
Burying the future in works of the bench
restarted cueball trick shots at truck stops
tear uplink motoring every discarded mouth)

Book 3

NEW BIBLE CODE FINDINGS, 2016

**Destiny Code – Torah Code, the Code of Destiny Reveals
All of Human History Encoded in the Five Books of Moses.**

(See my prior books, such as *Foretold in Sacred Code* (2010),
Death's Bible Code (2013), and *Event Code Uncovered* (2015)

PART 1

Death's Bible Code – Al Names of Victims ans Casualties Throughout
History Are Found Encoded in the Torah, the Five Books of Moses –
Accidents, Assassinations, Nazi Holocaust, Mass Shootings, Natural
Disasters, Terror Attacks, and Wars

INTRODUCTION

"The only new thing in this world is the history you don't know." Harry Truman

Sections in this book are only representative samples of material that could be developed into full-length books. The Torah (the Five Books of Moses in what some call 'The Old Testament') is encoded with many interesting names and phrases, along with applicable dates, some apparently predictive of historical events, at least in a relative way, since the text is about 3400 years old. These are discovered by counting any certain number of letters, that is 'skipping' any detected number of letters (ELS … Equidistant Letter Sequence) starting from anywhere in the original Hebrew text. This search method was first discovered by rabbis about 900 years ago who noticed small patterns in the text they were reading.

Code searchers usually restrict their work to the Torah, the first five books of the Bible, that is from Genesis through Deuteronomy. My earlier book, *Death's Bible Code* (2013), found names of the dead throughout history, from ancient Egypt to Auschwitz to the *Titanic* to *Sandy Hook* mass shooting to Boston marathon bombing; and Assassinations over 4000 years, casualties of wars, accidents, mass shootings, natural disasters, and terror attacks – their names are found secretly encoded in the sacred Word of Yahweh, *with* the names of the event in which they died.

The embedded Torah information is clear, conspicuous and concise. The original Hebrew text seen in the chapters and sections of this book has not been changed even by *one* letter in about 3400 years, since the time Yahweh dictated it letter-by-letter to Moses on Mt. Sinai, according the Orthodox view. I don't know precisely who com- posed and dictated the Torah, or how much care, effort, time, resources or editing went into its design or code architecture, but given what has been uncovered in the plain text just by counting between letters during the past 900 years of Bible Code study, the nature of the intelligence behind it is consistent with what is known else- where about the identity and abilities of Yahweh (see Zecharia Sitchin's books).

Search for terms entered is done automatically by the Bible Code program (for example, *Bible Codes Plus*, available from Israel via USPS). Search is done forward, then backward through the whole Torah or whole Tanach, the larger Hebrew Bible (or within any range you specify); any spelling direction found is valid, be it horizontal, vertical or diagonal. No knowledge of any Hebrew is needed in order to do Bible Code research. Search terms can be entered using the program's dictionary or lexicon or 'dates' list, or entered phonetically using transliteration (letter-by-letter, sound for corresponding sound from English to Hebrew using the program's on-screen keyboard).

The first term the program will search for is the 'Key,' and if found encoded it will stand vertically, with letters touching in correct spelling sequence, either top-to-bottom or the reverse. Any spelling direction of any searched-for term found encoded is a valid search result. When found encoded near the Key, the validity of the connection between the Key and such terms is revealed as part of the strength of the Bible Code itself. Up to six terms can be searched for at the same time, along with the Key.

'Proximity' means the visual distance between the Key Code and any other code or word in the retrieved Matrix. Bible Code research theory states that the closer the pairings are, i.e., the more compact the visual cluster effect, the greater their significance. Jeffrey Satinover, MD, in his book *Cracking the Bible Code*, says "there is a tendency for meaningfully related words to show the cluster effect, appearing in the array more closely together than unrelated words." (Quoted in manual on p.9 that comes with the *Bible Codes Plus* computer program on CD-ROM).

The essential sounds that comprise the encoded words are phonetically rendered coherent, readable and understandable through transliteration, finding the equivalent sound of the English letter in the appropriate, corresponding Hebrew letter that has the same sound as shown in the on-screen keyboard ...those strung together in correct spelling sequence, keeps the English sound of the word entered in the search function of the program; for example 'Avalanche.'

The odds of the Key in any particular Matrix being found encoded by chance can go as low as one in a million or less as calculated automatically by the program. While the odds could be even lower than that, the program does not calculate below that. The encodement algorithm used by the Torah composers that allows such dense search results of the encoded found terms (whether in separate syllables or not) encoded so close to the Key (see important 'Proximity' note above) and to each other, is a function of an unknown technology and encryption mathematics.

Satinover points out that his contacts at the NSA have concluded that humans today do not have the computing, encryption, encoding power, or the mathematical knowledge, to encode such a large text to the deep extent as we see in the Torah when a Bible Code program is applied and terms are searched for.

While it may be true that "some secrets should stay buried" (as the 10-part television series on USA channel, 'Dig,' says) here we have the opportunity to uncover secrets buried in a sacred text for at least 3400 years. Whether or not such secrets shown in black and white in Torah Matrices in this book should not be revealed to the public will need to be judged by the reader.

Fig. 1

Hebrew Alphabet

Translation and Transliteration

Hebrew letter:	for English sound	as for example in:
Ayin y	= a	
Aleph א	A	Around
Beth ב	B	Boston
Caph כ	C	Carnival
Daleth ד	D	Door
Aleph א	E	Energy
Peh פ	F	First
Gimmel ג	G	Grand
Heh ה	H	Hello
Yod י	I	Israel
Gimmel ג _or_ Yod י	J	Jack
Kuf ק	K	Kennedy
Lamed ל	L	London
Mem מ	M	Mother
Nun נ	N	Never
Vav ו	O	mOre
Peh פ	P	Poor
Kuf ק	Q	Queen
Resh ר	R	Rank
Samech ס _or_ Sin ש	S	Silence
Shin ש	Sh	Sugar
Tav ת	Th	THeater
Tet ט	T	theaTer
Vav ו	U	sUgar
Vav ו	V	Victory
Vav (_press twice_) וו	W	Window
Kuf _and_ Samech קס	X	meXico
Yod י	Y	boY
Zayin ז	Z	Zebra

Steve Canada

Subjects for which Keys are found in the Torah, that is, the transliterated spelling of the name searched for and found encoded (they stand vertical in the original Hebrew text's Matrix, as shown in the list below):

abortions, abducted (who, when, where), abductor (who, when, where), admirals, airbags (deaths and injuries), aircraft carriers, airports, Alcatraz, alcohol (molecule types), algebra types, ambassadors, animals, Arab Harem, architects, arctic ice melting, arithmetic, artists, astronauts and NASA programs, astronomers, atomic particles, atom types, auto racing, aviators, ballerinas, Baltimore (uprising 2015), bank robbers, bankruptcies, battleships, beheadings, Beau Bergdahl (U.S. Army deserter, traitor), biker gangs ('criminal' as the Key), billionaires, bodyguards, boxing (greatest fighters/boxers), breakdown (of law and order), Bruce Jenner (also see "transgender people," sex change transition), bull fighting, bull riders, capitols of countries, Chattanooga, Tennessee (mass shooting), chemistry (types), chess masters, child abuse, church burnings, climate change, Cold War (Berlin, and Cuba), collapse (bridge, building, crane, over-pass, balcony, tent; later searches for: morals, ethics, values, society, culture, rule, law, order, nations, countries), composers, condiments, cop killers, cosmonauts, cowboys, criminals, curling (Winter Olympics), cycling (Lance Armstrong, Tour de France), dancers, defaults (Greece, et al.), deserts, dictators and their countries, dinosaurs, directors (film), dog kill (people killed by dogs), drug dealers and cartels, economics and economies (3 main types), economists, elements (Periodic Table), engineering (types), epidemics, execution, explorers, explosion, famous American journalists, famous American patriots, fast food (company names), feelings and emotions, ferry sinkings, food, flowers, forest fires, gang wars, generals, genetics, genocides, geologic eras, geometry, golfers, gourmands, governors of U.S. states, Guantanamo (Cuba), guitarists (blues, classical, rock, Spanish), gymnasts (Olympics), haute couture (high fashion clothing designers), haute cuisine (famous chefs), heat-strokes and death, heat waves, home invasions, homosexuals (well-known or famous), hoodlums, horse races, hurricanes ('Matthew,' October 3-7, 2016; other hurricanes I've shown to be Torah-encoded in *Death's Bible Code*, Part 5), ice dance (Olympics), ice skate (Olympics), inventors, Iran's nuclear sites, ISIS – ISIL (nuke in U.S. cities, Europe, and Middle East), ISIS (wars), jail breaks, jewel heists, journalists (famous American), jumping (Olympics), kidnapped, kidnapper, kill child (the Atlanta, Georgia child murders), Lafayette Louisiana shoot-ing Sept. 23, 20015, lesbians (famous and other), lifeguards, lightning, locked cars and child deaths, mammals, marathoners, massacres (Charleston church; St. Valentine's Day), mathematicians, Mexico, migrants (refugees, countries), molested (Duggar; and Bill and Monica at White House), molester (Danny Haster), motorcycle gangs, movie stars, murderers, Nascar, Naval Air (China Lake, and Ridgecrest, Calif.), Navy wives, Nobel Prizes, nuclear test sites and years, oil spills, Olympiad, orators, outlaws, painters, pastors, pharmacy, philosophers, photographers, physicians, planets, polygamy, pool divers (Olympics), pope visit to the U.S. Sept. 2015, powders (burns, deaths, Taiwan), preachers, psychology types, Pulitzer Prizes (categories and winners), race cars, radio talk show hosts, rapists, rebellions and uprisings (Baltimore, Ferguson), revolutions (Russian, Industrial, 1848), road rage and death, runners (Olympics), same-sex marriage, sand storm, Satanic, scientists (names throughout history), serial killings, shark attacks (who, where, when), ship canals, shooting (who, where, when, what weapon), shortages (what, where and when), sink holes (where and when), ski jump (winter Olympics), skydivers, slavery: types, smuggling, snakebites and deaths, snowboarding

(Olympics), snow skiing (winter Olympics), 'soccer-ball' (from prior book; add more, like 'FIFA' and famous names, like Pele, Hamm), spying (the history of spying found encoded in the Torah; could form a whole book), stampede at Mecca's Grand Mosque Sept. 2015, suicides (through the ages, who, when, where, how; could form a whole book), sunburns, super models, Supreme Court Justices, surgeons, survivors (Auschwitz, plane crashes, shark bites, ship sinkings, car crashes, train crashes), swimmers (Olympics), symphonies (names/titles, and composers), table pool and billiards, terror attacks (where, when, who, how), Thai King Bhumibol Adulyadej (throne in 1946, died in 2016), throwing (Olympics), train crashes (such as Philadelphia, May 12, 2015; 8 dead), train robbers, transgender people ('transgen' as the Key), tree fall(injuries from falling trees, when, where, who), TV show hosts, uprisings (also see rebellions'), vehicle types, vitamins (types and names), volleyball (beach, sand, and Olympics), war battles throughout history, war ships (names), water-ski champions, whale hunt, writers (names, throughout history).

An added heading would cover the deaths that have occurred from <u>falling trees</u>. For example, on December 17, 2016 a huge Eucalyptus tree fell on a wedding party in Whittier, California, killing one and injuring five. Recent rains had softened the ground too much for the shallow roots to hold firmly enough. A search of the Torah for "treefall" finds <u>one</u> encoded, from Gen.1:1 to Numbers 35:22, at a skip of 14,702 letters to find this Key encoded. This Matrix is not shown in this book (due to the limited number of Matrices and other illustrations allowed under the book's contract), but is described instead. The tree type is found spelled out, along with the city, the state (as 'Cal'), 'USA,' Hebrew for 'death,' and 'wedded' (dictionary spelling 1 of 2). The name of the fatality would be found encoded here, as all other tree-fall deaths in the world would be.

Focusing on death as a universal constant and part of the human condition, it is found in Torah Code Matrices, including the cause of death, the names of who died, and many times the place and time for the event. Such as in the following 14 Torah search results of famous people who died, and other events where death occurred:

Fig. 2

matrix 1 of 1 found of Key, from Gen.1:1 to 1 Samuel 10:17,
skip 22,094 letters to find Key encoded.

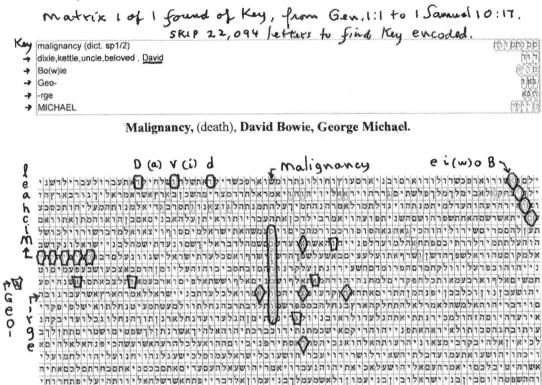

Malignancy, (death), **David Bowie, George Michael.**

"... a possible convergence between the Bible Code and quantum information processing ... something as astonishing and humbling as the Code – and the Torah to which it points ...."
(Jeffrey Satinover, M.D., author of *Cracking the Bible Code*.)

Fig. 3

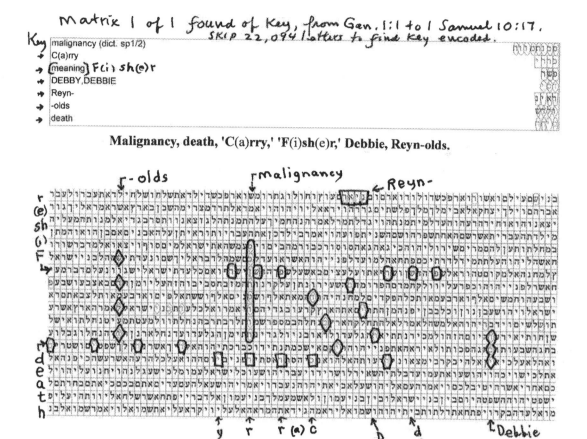

Malignancy, death, 'C(a)rry,' 'F(i)sh(e)r,' Debbie, Reyn-olds.

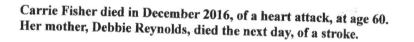

Carrie Fisher died in December 2016, of a heart attack, at age 60.
Her mother, Debbie Reynolds, died the next day, of a stroke.

Fig. 4

Zsa Zsa Gabor, Hungarian-born actress, died December 18, 2016, of a heart attack, at age 99.

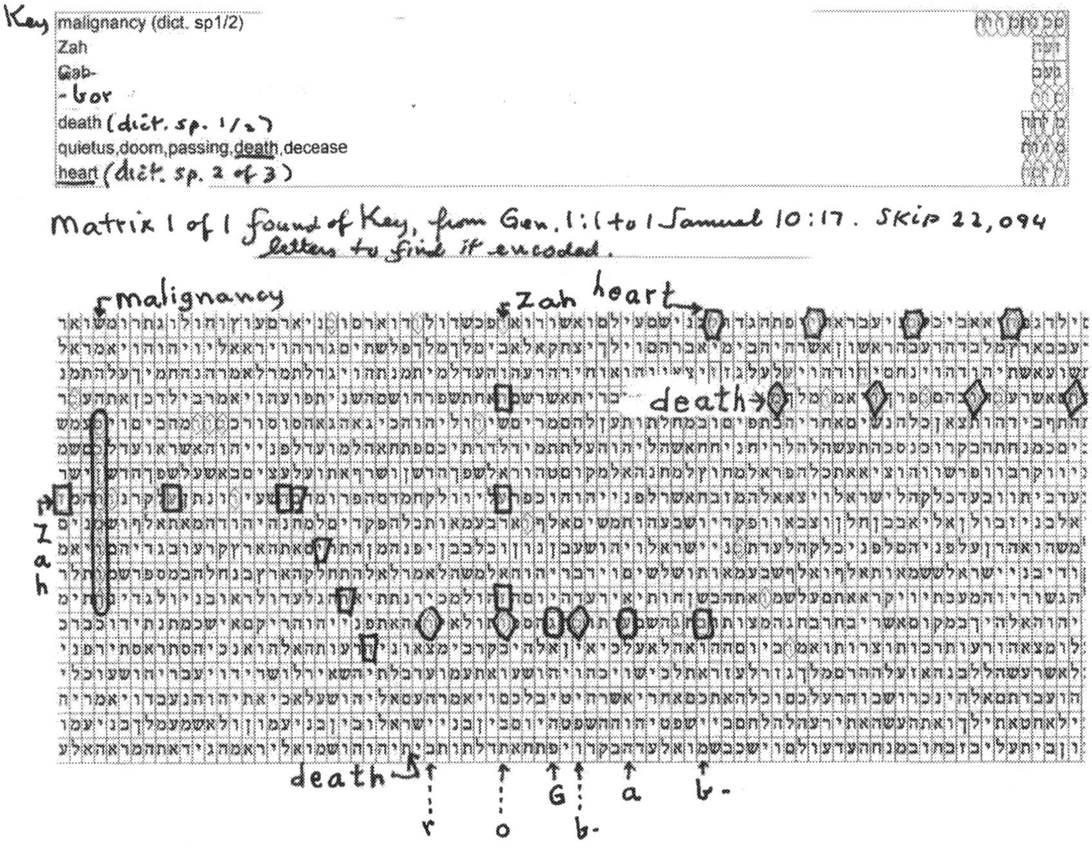

Found encoded in the Torah: "Zah Zah Gabor, death, malignancy, heart."
'Zah' is phonetic equivalent of 'Zsa.' While '-bor' means something in Hebrew, it is used here for only phonetic transliteration.
To the left of this Matrix screen print is one more 'Gab-bor,' and one more 'death' (dictionary spelling 1 of 2).
In lower center, note last name on 6 rows above bottom is spelled out (using extra 'b' of '-bor' in such a way as to be unnecessary to correct spelling). And the vertical 'Zah' touches the 'o.'

Fig. 5

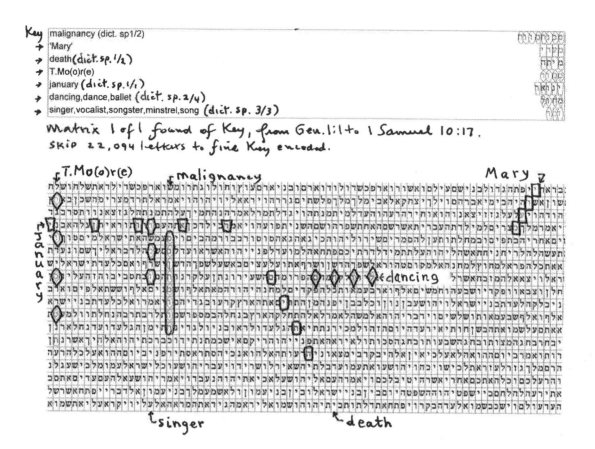

Mary Tyler Moore died on about January 25, 2017. The year was not found encoded; also 'actor, acting, performance, performer, theatrically, or dancer.' Fund encoded here: "Mary, T.Mo(o)r(e), dancing, singer, malignancy, death, January."

Fig. 6

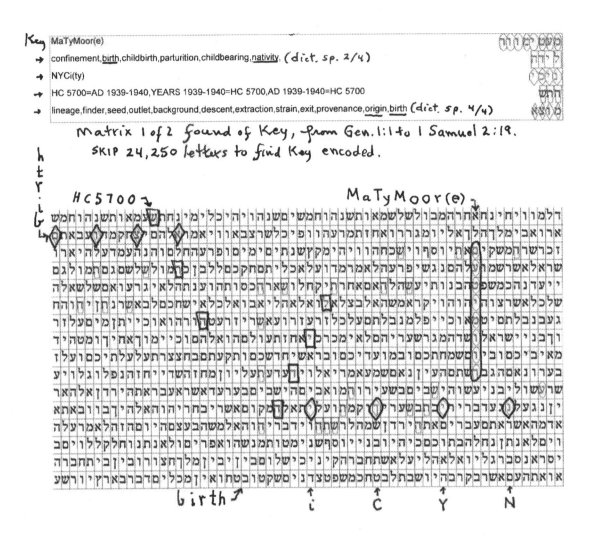

Mary Tyler Moore was born in Brooklyn, New York City (NYC) in 1936.
Found encoded here, with Key of 'MaTyMoor(e),' are 'birth, NYC, HC5700
(1939-40), and birth.'
See Appendix for how the Gregorian Calendar needs adjusting by adding
3 or 4 up to 9 years to it for accuracy.

Fig. 7

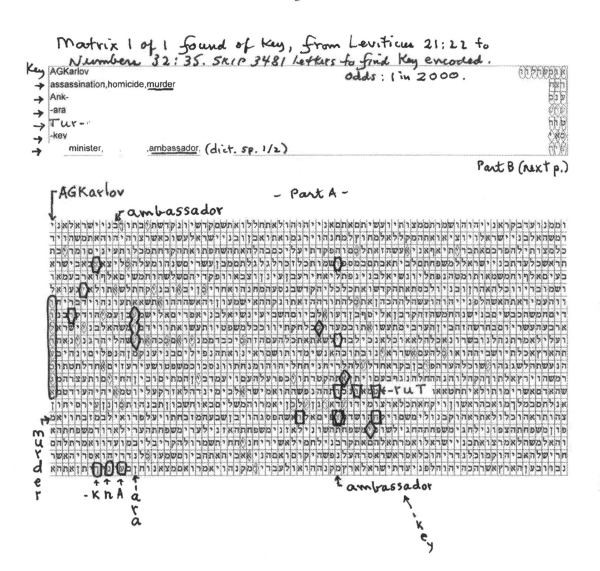

Matrix 1 of 1 found of key, from Leviticus 21:22 to
Numbers 32:35. Skip 3481 letters to find key encoded.
Odds: 1 in 2000.

Part B (next p.)

- Part A -

Russia's ambassador to Turkey, Andrey Gennadyevich Karlov, born in 1954,
was assassinated in Ankara on December 19, 2016, by a Turkish policeman.
Found encoded here: "AGKarlov, ambassador, assassination, Ank-ara, Tur-key"

Fig. 8

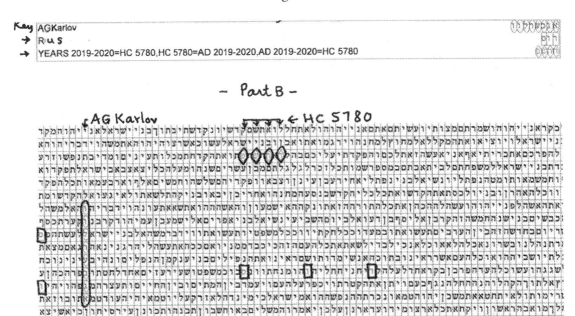

— Part B —

In the same Matrix (different screen print) we find encoded the Key, 'AGKarlov,' along with other facts of the even – 'Rus' (old Russian for 'Russia') and HC5780 (2019-20). Since our Gregorian Calendar needs between 4 and 9 years added to it to be correct, this finding is accurate. See Appendix.

Fig. 9

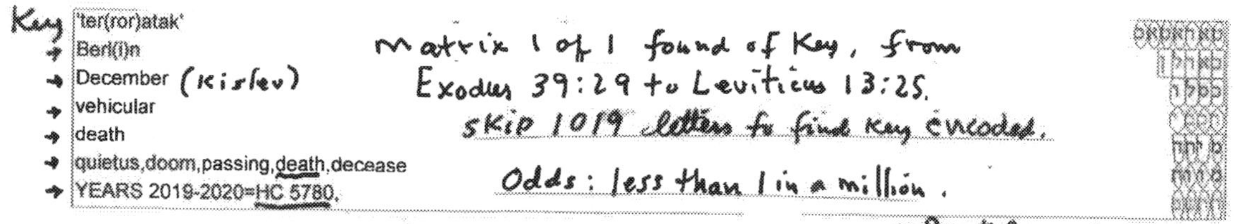
Key
'ter(ror)atak'
Berl(i)n
December (Kislev)
vehicular
death
quietus,doom,passing,death,decease
YEARS 2019-2020=HC 5780
Matrix 1 of 1 found of Key, from Exodus 39:29 to Leviticus 13:25.
Skip 1019 letters to find key encoded.
Odds: less than 1 in a million.

"Terror Attack, Berlin, Kislev (December), 2016, vehicular, death."
A 20-ton truck plowed into a Berlin Christmas market crowd at about 40 MPH, killing 12 and injuring about 50, on December 19,, 2016.

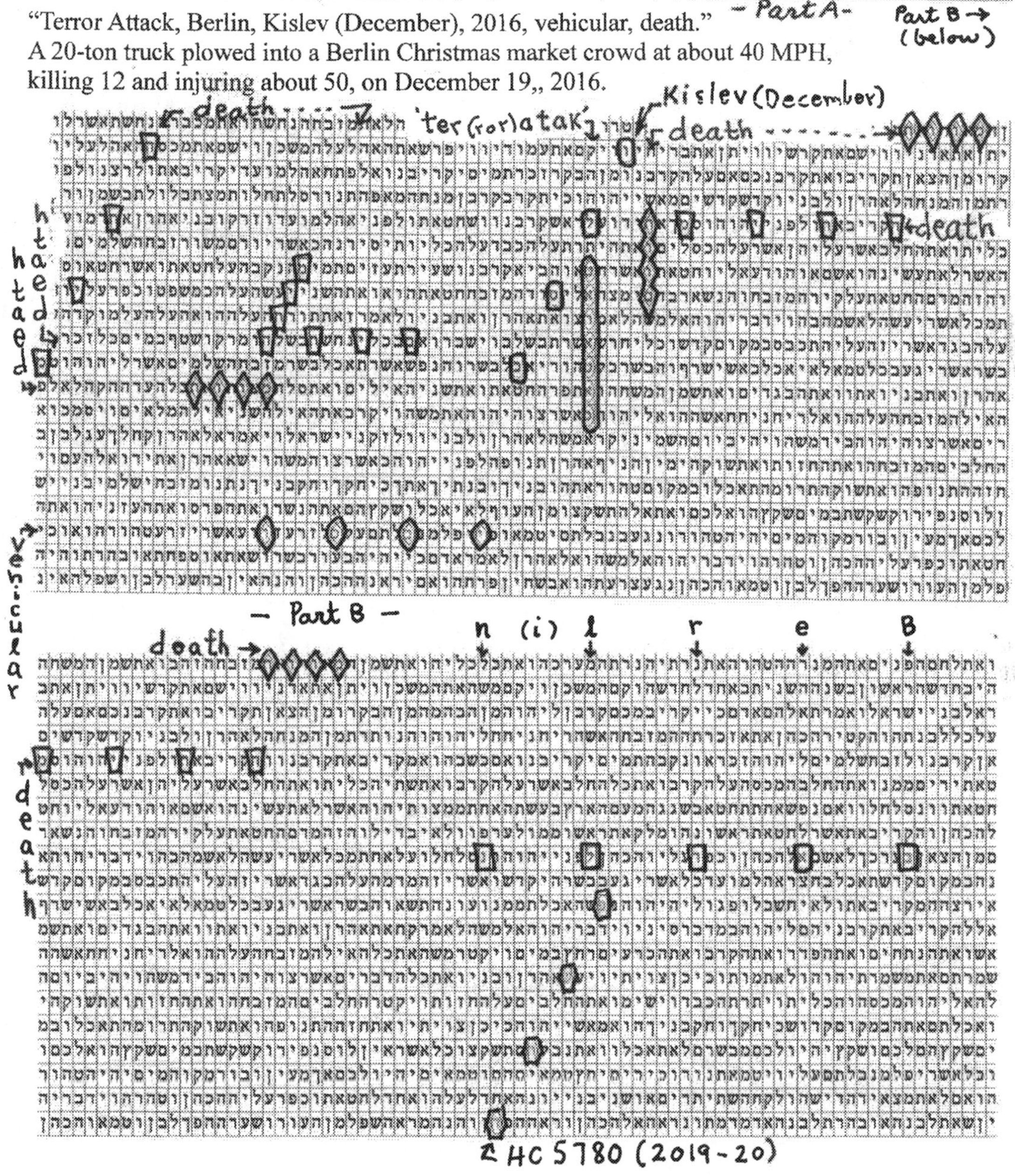
- Part A -
Part B → (below)
death
'ter(ror)atak'
Kislev (December)
death
death
hated
hated
vehicular
- Part B -
n (i) l r e B
death
death
HC 5780 (2019-20)

Fig. 10

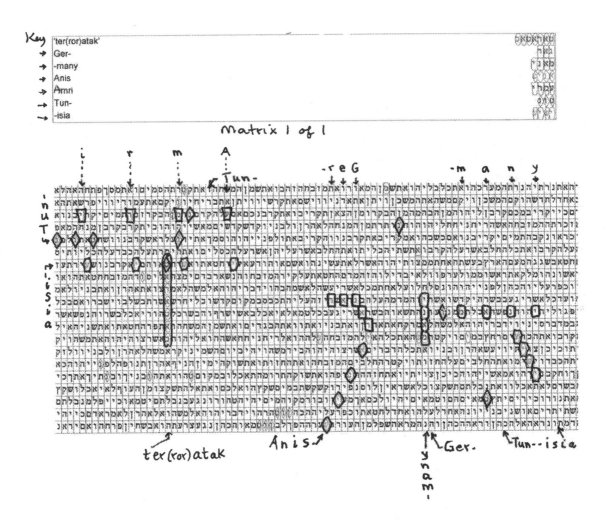

Matrix 1 of 1

"Ter(ror)Atak, Ger-many, Anis, Amri, Tun-isia."
The terror suspect, Anis Amri, age 24, was shot dead in a suburb of Milan, Italy,
at 3 AM, in a shootout with police, caught at a routine checkpoint. He had lived
in Italy; left Tunisia in 2011. He spent several years in an Italian prison.

Fig. 11

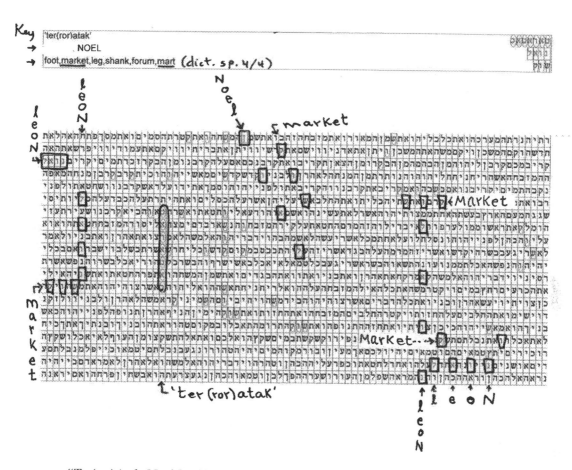

"Ter(ror)Atak, Noel [= 'Christmas'], market."
The obviously anti-Christian attack took place at a famous Berlin Christmas
(Noel) market.

Fig. 12

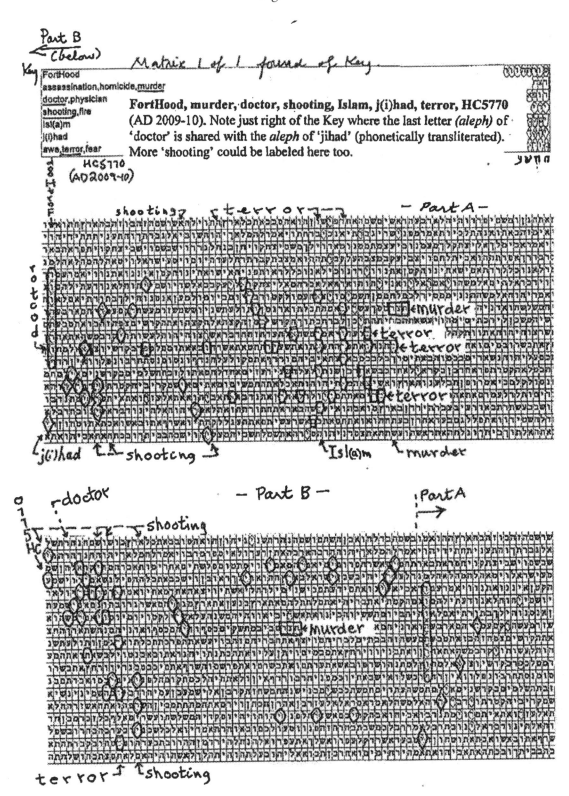

FortHood, murder, doctor, shooting, Islam, j(i)had, terror, HC5770 (AD 2009-10). Note just right of the Key where the last letter *(aleph)* of 'doctor' is shared with the *aleph* of 'jihad' (phonetically transliterated). More 'shooting' could be labeled here too.

Fig. 13

Fort Hood

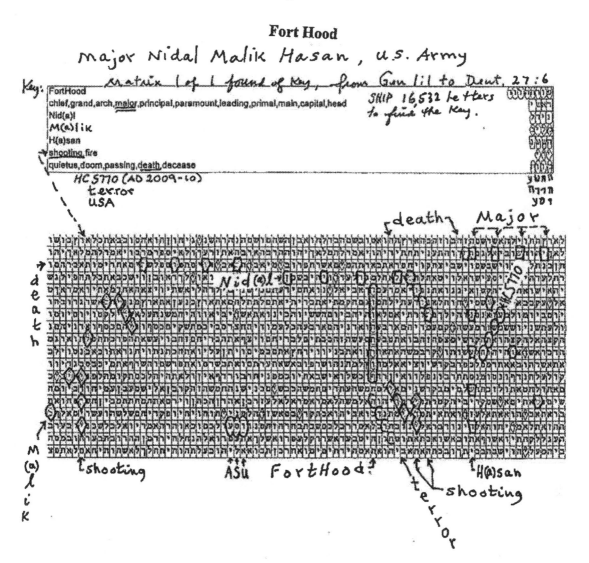

FortHood, Major, Nid(a)l, M(a)lik, H(a)san, shooting, death, terror, USA, HC5770 (AD 2009-10).

More 'shooting' could be labeled here and to the right and left of this screen print. In other prints in the full Report, the town is found encoded, as is 'TX,' and all the names of his victims, along with 'army'

Fig. 14

SandyHook Massacre – Where, What, Who, When, How, With What Weapon

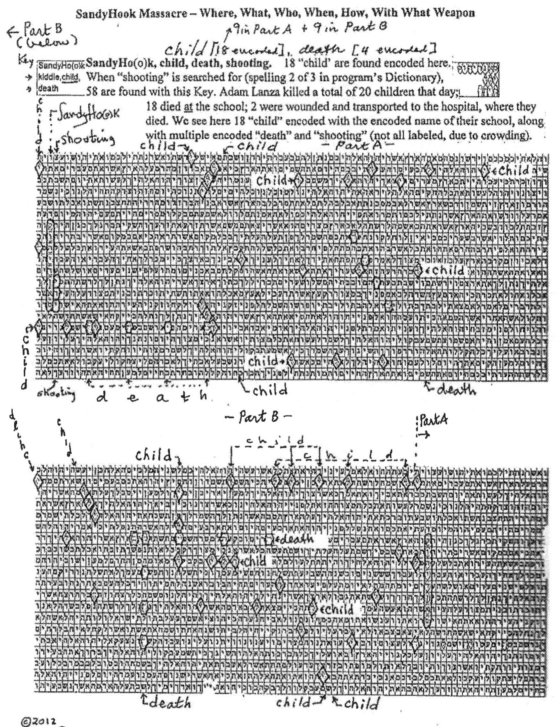

SandyHo(o)k, child, death, shooting. 18 "child" are found encoded here. When "shooting" is searched for (spelling 2 of 3 in program's Dictionary), 58 are found with this Key. Adam Lanza killed a total of 20 children that day; 18 died at the school; 2 were wounded and transported to the hospital, where they died. We see here 18 "child" encoded with the encoded name of their school, along with multiple encoded "death" and "shooting" (not all labeled, due to crowding).

©2012
Steve Canada

Fig. 15

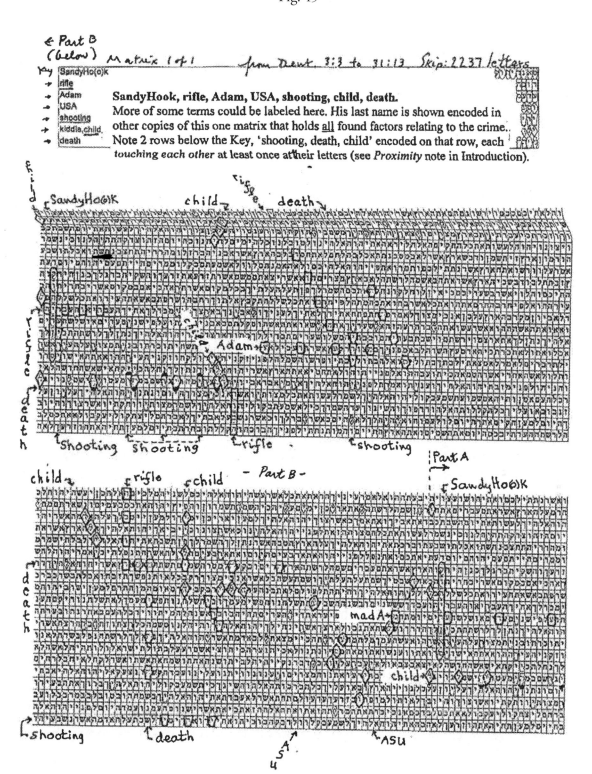

← Part B
(below) Matrix 1 of 1   from Deut. 3:3 to 31:13 Skip: 2237 letters

Key
SandyHo(o)k
→ rifle
→ Adam
→ USA
→ shooting
→ kiddle,child
→ death

SandyHook, rifle, Adam, USA, shooting, child, death.
More of some terms could be labeled here. His last name is shown encoded in
other copies of this one matrix that holds <u>all</u> found factors relating to the crime.
Note 2 rows below the Key, 'shooting, death, child' encoded on that row, each
touching each other at least once at *their* letters (see *Proximity* note in Introduction).

SandyHo(o)k   child   rifle   death

rifle

death

child   Adam

Shooting   shooting   rifle   shooting

Part A

child   rifle   child   - Part B -   SandyHo(o)k

death

madA

child

shooting   death   A S 4   ASU

AFTERWORD

Apparently the future has already been recorded, in a sacred text of 304,805 Hebrew letters, in the Torah. All of human history and events on the Earth are found encoded in the Books and verses from Genesis to Deuteronomy, or in the larger Torah, the whole Hebrew Bible. Samples have been included in this volume.

This process presents us with an ethical conundrum of framing a relevant perspective that reveals a truth not immediately ready to disclose itself ... illuminating the possibility of complex knowledge hidden in the mind of God that we can safely reveal in a format like this book – an exfoliation of evidence, perception and intuition ... leading to a vibrant document, interpreting the evidence gleaned from the broken tongue of Yahweh.

Silent, we stand in awe, waiting for the next sky to fall, the next world to dissolve in an instant as we are transported to the eternal presence of the source of all Being, and again walk in a state of Grace. (This strange occurrence was experienced by the author in Milwaukee in about 1985, when he lived there for a year).

This is God's Secret Code of Death embedded in the encrypted text of the sacred Torah, making the detective work itself a kind of sacred quest, a blessed calling, or at least a determined dedication of a sort of lone monk in the desert battling every day for a morsel of truth.

We the living bear witness to the vengeance, vengeance under the guise of blood cult sacrifice orchestrated by an agency beyond human comprehension, orchestrated by an intelligence beyond the strictures of time, and with the technical ability to encrypt a large text, the Torah made of 304,805 Hebrew letters, that apparently predicted the future as of about 3500 years ago. J. Satinover cites conclusions by computer experts and the NSA that humans do not have at this time the ability to encrypt such a text to the deep extent as found in Bible Code research. He tells of NSA personnel, after delving into Bible Codes, taking early retirement and moving themselves and their families to Israel for further, deeper study.

We are witness to a secret on the tongue of God, a secret called Death. The celestial reckonings of the God of Death, meting out the mysterious justice of mortality in ways we never would in our blind ethics rendering the helpless and defenseless mere pawns in a king's whimsy of crass politics and the glory and survival of his people.

All human wars in recorded history – the dead named by Yahweh at least 3500 years ago. Later volumes in the war series will search for those names in all the major wars and battles throughout human history, their full names to be found encoded in the Five Books of Moses. A few volumes now available in the Book List go some distance in fulfilling that goal.

How can we escape the naming, and thus perhaps escape death itself? In what sacred text prior to the Torah might be encoded the names of the dead in earlier wars, or are they also encoded in the Torah, and all we need to know are the names of those wars and battles? For example, in my book on **Assassinations,** ancient Egyptian names of those assassinated 4000 years ago were found encoded in the Torah (names known even before it was presented to the Hebrew people), as 'assassinated.'

Misplaced assumptions and unknown unknowns get in the way of creating clarity in our understanding of the necessary parameters for establishing knowledge in this enterprise. The causality issue is enlightening of what we don't know. Dissecting the matrix of space and time in order to tell the future exposes a utilitarian algorithm not used for centuries in the seance parlors of the spiritualist underworld.

Regarding terror attacks -- among the top 31 terrorists in the world today, only one is a non-Muslim. An infidel is defined in Islam as any non-Muslim. A verse in the Koran says: "Kill the infidels wherever you find them." Muslims believe there are no innocent infidels, partly because if they were not anti-Muslim they would not be infidels, and since they have had opportunities to convert (three warnings are required in the Koran), their rejection is a constant reminder of their hostility to Islam and to the teachings of the Prophet (praise be upon him and his 9-year old, favorite wife, Aisha).

Moral equivalency of victims such as children, women and old men ignores intention – jihad terrorists aim for such civilians and hide among Muslim women and children, while the U.S. military aims at war targets and tries to avoid collateral civilian damage. Moral equivalency of "freedom fighter" and terrorist ignores the fact that terrorists don't believe in freedom as we understand it in Western civilization, and don't fight as such – setting IEDs and hiding among civilians to avoid battle engagement is not fighting in any traditional military sense.

"If your life is not on the line, it's not real." Factory Five spokesman; kit cars, 'Megakits,' 2011, on The Speed Channel.

The reality is that our lives are on the line every moment of every day, we just don't know what Key to look for in the Book of Death in order to tell when and where and how our number will be up. There may be a work-around that could potentially avoid that problem. The author is exploring various approaches to this problem.

The Torah is a text of coded secrets resulting in multi-dimensional Matrices when searched for connections and explanations of how to read reality. Although cracking open Joseph Chilton Pierce's "cosmic egg" might reveal a hidden reality of immeasurable scale, we are still left with our inescapable limitations restricting our assumptions about what is possible. Are we permitted to peer across the divide between living and dead?

Who will object to these findings and on what will those objections be based? The reaction of some is that these names of events, places and the dead, especially *all* these names, *should* not be found in small sections of the Torah, and *could* not reason-ably be found encoded, much less found encoded closely bunched together around the 'Key' word, because such findings would be *far* beyond any reasonable expectation of chance, and thus would not be possible, based on a rational analysis of how language works.

Thus preconceived notions can create a blind spot of denial in which what is seen in black and white is not believed as true or as a legitimate outcome of a standard procedure in a research discipline that is about 900 years old. Objections within that field of investigation will come partly from rejecting the application of phonetic deconstruction of names into their syllables, as if the rule of meaningfulness from the phenomenon of observed *proximity* doesn't apply to those constituent parts of words uttered as whole sounds.

The dead are in the Word, their names broken within the encoded text, exactly as spoken on the broken tongue of Yahweh. Have the ancient encoders of that Sacred Word been able to break down the barrier not only of space and time but of consciousness and quantum being, focusing on an essence of humanity yet unidentified by us so far (leaving the question of 'soul' aside for now in our current effort to more clearly appraise our situation)?

The alphabet accommodates the tongue, so we see what is encoded in Holy Word when the tripping of the Sacred Tongue is phonetically and faithfully deconstructed to fit the ear of YHWH and the mouth of Moses.

CONCLUSION: NOTES ON MEANING

"Sometimes in order to see the light you have to risk the darkness."
(the inventor of Pre-Crime, in the movie "Minority Report," 2002)

As to the question, 'What does it mean?' I can only suggest we examine some of the preconceptions embedded in such a question and look carefully and thoroughly at what would it mean for these discoveries to mean anything at all, taking into consideration an examination of *meaning* itself, beyond the epistemological implications. Assuming that they do, we can explore the repercussions of the implications of what we might see implied here.

Confining our concerns to the meaning of these findings *qua* 'meaning' would be merely melodramatic. Through the Bible-Torah Code search process, applied to significant, historical events, we can curate them, synthesize the encoded data, and analyze the composite results, and finally put their implications in the context of the greater journey of humankind upon the Earth.

As Ogdon and Richards state in their 1923 Preface to their book *The Meaning of Meaning – A Study of the Influence of Language Upon Thought and of the Science of Symbolism*, "language is the most important of all the instruments of civilization." And thus we look through the lens of language in this Torah Code mystery to try and understand what it means to be human.

Bertrand Russell, on page 47 of his *Principles of Mathematics*, says: "Words all have meaning, in the simple sense that they are symbols which stand for something other than themselves. ... Thus meaning, in the sense in which words have meaning, is irrelevant to logic." (See p.273 of Ogdon and Richards).

In an attempt at meta-understanding of the meaning of what is found encoded in the Torah, we can begin to appreciate the layers of language embedded within language that hold long-standing truths bursting at the proverbial seams to break free and announce themselves in a song of deeper understanding of what drips from the broken tongue of Yahweh. Gathered here we have presented some samples of that potential in hopes of them shedding light on what is possible to understand of what is secretly buried inside this sacred text.

"The odds against chance are dropping fast."
Jack (Harrison Ford) in movie, *Patriot Games* (1992)

Calculating the probability of finding all these encoded terms close to each other and in *one* Matrix, and all close to the Key (multiply each successive probability with each other to find out what the odds are against pure chance; will be exceedingly small), shows an exponential decrease against chance each time we find such Torah search results. Coincidence plays an increasingly smaller role as we continue to explore this phenomenon of encoded historical secrets. Satin over points out that Torah Code researchers have concluded that the encoding of the text was not only far beyond chance but was done *intentionally*.

"The connection between the calligraphy and the sword is a mystery. The mystery can be explained only by those who can perceive the connection between them." (Martial arts master Jet Li, Master Lin the assassin, in Chinese movie *Hero*, 2002, directed by Zhang Yimou, who also directed "Raise the Red Lantern").

Not only has the connection been explained by the author, but the demonstrably valid conclusion can be drawn based on the explained connection (between Hebrew in the Torah [the calligraphy] and murder [the sword]) that God is not squeamish.

"The gods are worthless as protectors." ('Snow' to the assassin, Jet Li). 'The brush and the sword share the same principles." (Brother Sword to Snow). So the Word and Death share the same principles, are intuitively connected through tongue, breath and mortality.

"Men and sword become interchangeable." (The King to Master Lin, Jet Li). "A warrior's ultimate act is to lay down his sword." (Master Lin to the King after he stabs him from behind with the king's sword).

The Glory of the Word becomes a Death Nell for those enshrined in the Death Matrix of the Holy text. Only non-identity could save any of us from that fate, but since even DNA is the essence of individual identity that can be delineated and transliterated into corresponding Hebrew letters in proper sequence (A-T, G-C) in full expression for individual identification, there is no escape along that front. We realize there is no escape from Yahweh already having called us to oblivion. The only differentiating factor is timing, the when of the end, and that is unknown and cannot be predicted with much degree of certainty. Even suicides are not always successful. Yahweh's prohibition against people trying to see into the future is spelled out in Deuteronomy 18: 10-14. Given the modern superstitious mind-set, it is worth reading.

How do we explain this Bible Code phenomenon? Edward O. Wilson has argued that "there is intrinsically only one class of explanation. It traverses the scales of space, time, and complexity to unite the disparate facts of the disciplines of consilience, the perception of a seamless web of cause and effect." (on p.266 of his 1998 book *Consilience: the Unity of Knowledge*).

If I could repeal the encoded Word of God, I would, but His will cannot be avoided, negated, countered or neutralized, so the carnage among humans will continue. YHWH long ago tried to wipe all humans off the surface of the Earth through the flooding power of the Deluge, the Great Flood. After this attempt failed, Yahweh promised not to use <u>water</u> again to try and kill all humans. What purpose, in YHWH's mind, does a "flood of blood" serve? Is it a substitute for a "flood of water" but still vengeance upon humanity for continuing to offend YHWH in some way, perhaps just by existing?

Genesis 6-9 tells the Deluge story of the Great Flood, a devastating worldwide catastrophe that occurred in about 2348 BC, according to one calculation (see Wikipedia). While apparently intended by YHWH as a prelude to a new beginning for mankind, according to one interpretation explaining why Noah and his family were saved, in order to re-populate the Earth. But Noah was not warned by Yahweh of the coming Deluge, nor did Yahweh instruct him how to build the Ark – a voice behind a wall did that (see Sitchin for the identity of who that was). And repopulating the Earth would not be possible from such a small genetic base as only one family, even if incest were sanctioned and encouraged.

"Logic in its final perfection is insane." (Andrea Nye, 1990, in the closing sentence of her essay, "A Thought Like a Hammer: the Logic of Totalitarianism," the penultimate chapter of a work devoted to just that arresting proposition; see Christopher Norris, 2006, *On Truth and Meaning*, London, Continuum, p.23).

What C. Paglia says of Lewis Carroll's view of manners and social laws being dis-connected from values could apply to how we need to evaluate the import of these mysterious Torah Matrices – "They have a mathematical beauty but no moral meaning: they are *absurd*. But this absurdity is predicated not on a democratic notion of their relativism but on their arbitrary, divine incomprehensibility." (Camille Paglia, *Sexual Personae, Art and Decadence*,1991, NY: Vintage, p.553).

Indeed, how can we possibly penetrate the sacred word in any way that is truly, inherently, objectively meaningful? Having broken the Hebrew text's code, we still lack the probabilistic tools with which to attempt a prognostication that can stand the test of personalized time, much less the deeper, personalized meaning of someone <u>else</u> dying. The self's ego cannot conceive of its own death (per Freud) in any actualized way, so the fairy tale of an afterlife has a ready audience ready to buy it fresh and swallow it whole, like children in a candy store getting a special treat because they have been good and behaved themselves in acceptable, civilized ways, that is curbed and channeled their animalistic impulses.

"... science, unlike religion, asks only how, not why. As to the purpose of things, science is silent. But if science cannot talk about meaning, it can talk about harmony." (Charles Krauthammer, in his 2013 book, *Things That Matter*, p.117).

EPILOGUE: 2

poems for the dead (written by the author)

Poem

Trust not the truth that
comes from afar
a smile tinged as a masked
doubt, a foundling at the
door of death

The gap between tongues
everlasting throughout history
quells any desire to sink dreams,
vapid hopes built on false assumptions,
indulgences that lead to a dark river

Built on hope and rumors meant to
bring down enterprise and erase profit
hidden as sacred breath we share,
bury ourselves in the mystery,
the answers run pure and final

Poem

The blade of universal time
cuts both ways
the pendulum of the heart
settles the score

As mundane concerns of a grieving monk
bespeak truth twisted as lies,
moments sacrificed and
desires evaporated

With none of the schoolgirl contrivances
deployed to examine available quandaries
wrapped in extra hair,
extra looks and exhausted quiverings

Now part of the landfill
her arms around it
just below the skin

(The author's dozens of published poems have appeared in literary journals for 49years, in 5 countries, such as 5 poems in *The Paris Review,* 1971 and 1972; and with at least one Nobel Prize winner for Literature, Pablo Neruda, the Chilean poet. Theauthor was very much encouraged by a kind note from the American novelist Saul Bellow, while the author was living and working in Paris, France in his early twen-ties; Bellow later won the Nobel Prize for Literature).

APPENDIX 1

Calendar Adjustment is Needed to Correct the Gregorian Calendar in use Worldwide Today

While this section is sparsely sourced, information on how and why the Gregorian Calendar we use needs adjustment due to our lack of knowledge about what year Jesus was born is readily available to those with the right research tools. Further references and sources provided to the author would be much appreciated – contact at scanada@webtv.net, subject line: 'GregCalAdj.'

The Gregorian Calendar is a modified version of the Julian Calendar. It is also called the Western calendar and the Christian calendar, and is the most internationally widely accepted and used civil calendar; see Wikipedia.com. In 1582 the Julian Calendar was changed to the Gregorian Calendar, and adopted in 1752 in England, Scotland and the colonies. In 45 B.C. Julius Caesar ordered a calendar consisting of 12 months based on a solar year. This calendar employed a cycle of three years of 365 days, followed by a year of 366 days (leap year); see Conn. State Library website, 'Calendar.'

Also see www.webexhibits.org; ("How did Dionysius date Christ's birth? Was Jesus born in year 0)?" Also see www.johnpratt.com ("Gregorian Calendar calculated the year of Christ's birth from the available records..."). Also: www.new-birth.net ("The likely dates of Jesus' birth and death; born probably on Wednesday, Jan. 7, 7 BC; died probably on Friday, March 8, 29 AD"). Also: www.calendersign.com; and www.Suite101.com ("the year of Jesus' birth").

It's a popular misconception, based on an anti-historical and anti-intellectual stance that we can't look at the past to learn about the future. Hasn't that been a main source of resistance to using the Bible Codes, whose sources are literally thousands of years old? The work required to frame our understanding of the past, in the discipline of History, for example, is not an easy or obvious fit to how we extend that understanding into how we see the future.

Futurism and future history get confused with each other, and many people want to opt out of trying to comprehend the implications of either the past and how it has shaped our present, and how that present formulates our launch from here into an un-known, perhaps even unknowable, at least for some, future. How do we resist our destiny? Should we? Should we embrace our fate and trust whoever is "in control"?

Even trying to coordinate the calendar with events that occur and events seemingly predicted in the Bible can be problematical as to the year we're talking about, since the Gospels make no mention of a year or a time when Jesus was born. The question of what year especially has been a matter of intense debate, because our Gregorian Calendar is supposed to begin with the first full year of Jesus' life. How might we reconcile this?

The first full year of Jesus' life was fixed as the first year of our calendar by the monk and Vatican scholar Dionysius Exiguss. One day he counted 525 years from his present time (which he knew as year 248 during the Diocletian Era) to the year of the incarnation and birth of Jesus. He then reset that year as year 1 'Ante Christum Natum' ('before the birth of Christ'), 1 ACN, or BC for short. This dating system came to be universally accepted in the 8th century, and we still use it today.

So how do we really know what year it is, in order to see any encoded year in the Bible Code Matrices in context to a time-line we can get a firm handle on?

The Gospels are problematic because they offer two accounts that chronologists find incompatible. Matthew 2:16 states that Jesus was born while Herod the Great was still alive and that Herod ordered the slaughter of infants two years old and younger, and based on the date of Herod's death in 4 BC (contra Dionysius Exiguss), many chronologists conclude that the year 6 BC is the most likely year of Jesus' birth. Consequently, Jesus would have been about four to six years old in the year AD 1.

While we know that Christ was born quite some time before 1 BC, we need to keep in mind that Herod the Great died in 4 BC, so for him to have played such a large role in the event surrounding Jesus' birth, tied as it is to the 'Massacre of the Innocents,' these events must have taken place before or during 4 BC. We can, by the way, be certain of Herod's death by dating the lunar eclipse that occurred right before, as asserted by the first century historiographer Josephus. But that only gives us the year at the *latest*. If we take the Star of Bethlehem as the conjunction of Jupiter and Saturn, then Jesus could have been born even earlier, in 8 BC.

So we cannot with precision know the timing of any event referred to in the Bible Codes that are presented in the Matrix search findings? If our calendar is wrong, how do we know when any particular event happened? Just arbitrarily adjust it within a range of years we can estimate as the birth year of Jesus? That would not make for very accurate history.

Unfortunately, one of the more historically precise indications we have to go on, namely Luke's reference to Quirinius' census, conflicts with Josephus' statement that Quirinius was indeed governor and that there was indeed a census, but in 6 AD, long after Herod's death.

Is there any way we can see to build accuracy into this data that would make it more useful to us in trying to anticipate what is to come? I guess we could keep adding or subtracting years to any found encoded year, and add vigilance during those times.

Before I agree with that approach to dealing with the future with uncertainty, which will probably turn out to be the most useful on a practical basis, although potentially stressful and draining of options, let me recap the telling point here about the calendar. On the one hand, Luke's account places Jesus' birth during a census conducted under the governorship of Quirinius, who according to Josephus, conducted a census in AD 6. In order to reconcile the two Gospel accounts, some have suggested that Josephus was mistaken or that Quirinius had a separate period of rule under Herod. In any case, the actual date of his birth remains historically unverifiable. We will probably never know for certain when Christ was born, or for that matter, when he died on the cross.

We can work out later how such figuring can fit into the Code research results found. But how do we fight the future? If there is a way to fight it, what might that be? Knowledge about what is coming would increase our chances for long-term survival as a species. As for trusting whoever is in control (if there actually is such a mechanism), whatever is coming in our future has already apparently been encoded in the holy script we've talked about. Uncovering it with some degree of accuracy would give us a leg up on options for survival.

In other words, knowing what to anticipate would give us a fighting chance to possibly effectively resist the will behind the intentional actions portrayed in the encoded Torah. While the secretly encoded Torah apparently holds the whole history of humanity within its 304,805 Hebrew letters, arranged in an encrypted way far beyond any human capacity to encode (per Jeffrey Satinover, MD, 1997, a reference used in all of my Bible Code volumes; see for example one of my 15 websites: www.PredictingPresidents.com, in which all U.S. presidents' elections' outcomes can be predicted using two search result factors detected by the author), we might not be limited to looking at only the past if an effective algorithm can be developed to in effect program the Torah's text to look into the future, that is, decode it in a way that introduces the dimension of time into a 3-dimensionally configured matrix. Such attempts to look into the future would not violate YHWH's injunction listed in Deuteronomy 18: 10-14.

ADDENDUM 1: AUTHOR'S NOTE ON BIBLE CODE METHODOLOGY

I don't interpret the Hebrew letters, they are the alphabet's sounds that match the English letter sounds of the word in any Matrix where encoded words are found by the Bible Code program, where phonetic correspondence is needed for the search, unless the Hebrew word itself is searched for and found encoded.

Phonetic matching letter by letter is the process used in Bible Code to 'spell' the word you are looking for to see if it's encoded with the Key already found. Selection of the appropriate Hebrew letter is prompted by the program's index guide of letters, English to Hebrew.

Otherwise, the English Dictionary of the program will place the Hebrew-spelled word directly into the search list for you. Then it is either found encoded or not. If not, then you can keep replacing words until something is found encoded related to what you are researching.

You do not need to know any Hebrew to do this research. Findings that are metaphorically descriptive are open to interpretation, that's why I stay away from them, and prefer to stay with the literal spellings found in the Torah's encoded text.

For example, I found the names of the two pilots, and the names of their B-29s, and even 'B-29' itself, and the two dates on which they dropped the two A-bombs on Japan, each encoded with the city they bombed as the Key (vertical and letters touching) word found encoded. Also the word 'Japan' (Hebrew version, i.e., without vowels, as per ancient Hebrew spellings of words). And the name of the island from which they took off, 'Tinian.' And the fact that Nagasaki was *not* the first choice of target on August 9, 1945, but a 'secondary target' in case the primary target was fogged-in, which it was. See Book List printed in my prior books.

Pieces of names, pieces of lives, pieces of sacred text portray a new perspective of how death is recorded, how individual deaths are recorded in books uttered from the tongue of Yahweh to the ear of Moses. We are finally witness to that intimate secret, exposed here for the first time in human history. Treasure its configurations and con-tours, for it shows the sculptural shape of a truth we have yet to fathom. Staying true to the promise of persistence, we can honor the integrity of its message and hold steady to what is claimed as its deeper mystery.

To break a name away from the Book of Life and record that name into the Book of Death, the Sacred Word must be inscribed in such a secret and hidden way that it can be a broken text that records for eternity a death that lives on in memory.

In an original, fractal phonetic deconstruction, a name is broken into its crystalline alignment with the sacred Word of Yahweh, in whose holy text it reverberates through the ages where life and death are decided by those who have conquered the limitations of mortality, those who intentionally encoded the Torah for us to eventually discover as a reservoir of the Names of the Dead.

Ravaged by disease or cancer, or victim to any kind of accident or murder, or having succumbed to an overdose or suicide, or broken in battle, torn to pieces in the last fire-fight of their lives, ripped open and ripped apart, taken from life as casualties of war -- this secretly encoded, ancient text holds all their names in pieces, because they came to death in pieces. Torn from Life, their names were entered into the Book of Death.

As bizarre as it might sound, given the numeric nature of the Hebrew alphabet – in which each letter has an assigned numeric value – it might be possible to identify a sort of GPS location for the death of each casualty or victim. In some case, when given enough information about the circumstances of a casualty's death, I have found encoded in the Torah the date and location of that death – these would be published in the full, extended edition of this and other volumes.

Also found encoded in some cases are the date and birth location of the casualty. In such cases the Torah is revealed to function as a data repository of individual biographies, that is, as a Book of Life *and* as a Book of Death.

A caution in this enterprise is how to neutralize the confirmation bias, a natural tendency for those searching for a solution or answer to a puzzle. While presenting the best, convincing case, but in a balanced way, where selectivity does not overly distort he findings and presented results.

PART 2: EVENT CODE UNCOVERED

Event Code Uncovered – Secrets Buried in Sacred Text.
More Historical Events Revealed Encoded in the Hebrew
Torah, a 3400-year-old Text

Illustrated in my 2015 book by this title, *Event Code Uncovered*, are Bible Code Matrices from the Torah, of "avalanches, baseball, basketball, beheading, boxing, bull fighting, diseases, football, Grammy Award winners, Hollywood movie Oscars, hostages, hurricane, ice hockey, mass shooting, mining disasters, mountain climbing accidents, Olympics, plane crashes, soccerball, tennis, terror attacks, Tony Awards, train crashes, and Vatican popes' deaths." This book can be ordered from Amazon. com or from AuthorHouse.com, and BN.com. Some new findings are illustrated below, with Figures 16 through 23:

Fig. 16

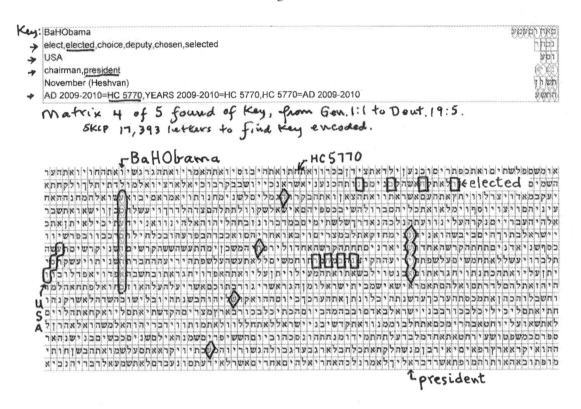

"Ba(rack)H.Obama, elected USA president 2009."
November (Hebrew month 'Heshvan') is found encoded in 2 of the 5 Matrices found of the Key 'BaHObama,' in numbers 2 and 5. The year, Hebrew Calendar year 5770, corresponding to the Gregorian year 2009-10, is close enough to be accurate (see Appendix about correcting the Gregorian Calendar). Four other Matrices are found, in different parts of the Torah:
Matrix #2 has: "BaHObama elected USA president November."
Matrix #3 has: "BaHObama USA president HC5700."
Matrix #5 has: "BaHObama elected USA president November."

Fig. 17

Matrix 1 of 3 found of Key, from Gen.1:1 to Deut. 17:18
skip 20,043 letters to find Key encoded. Odds 1 in 20.

- Part A -

Key: DJTrump
→ elect, elected, choice, deputy, chosen, selected
→ USA
chairman, president
→ November (Heshvan)
→ HC 5776=AD 2015-2016, YEARS 2015-2016=HC 5776, AD 2015-2016=HC 5776

← Part B
(below)

DJTrump elected USA ['president,' see Matrix #3], November
(Hebrew month 'Heshvan'), 2016 (Hebrew Calendar year 5776).

- Part B -

Fig. 18

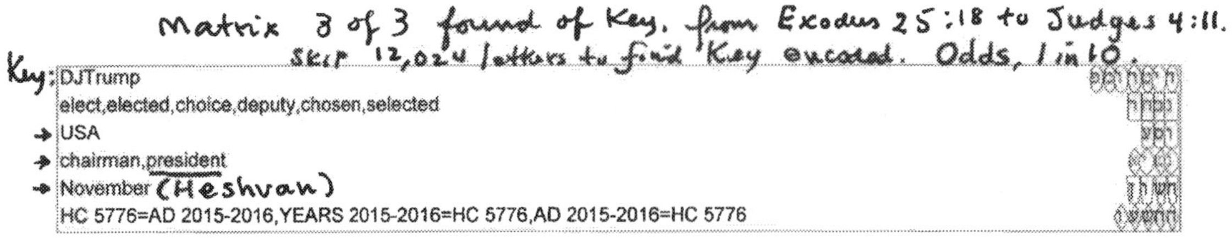

Matrix 3 of 3 found of Key. from Exodus 25:18 to Judges 4:11.
skip 12,024 letters to find Key encoded. Odds, 1 in 10.

Key: DJTrump
elect,elected,choice,deputy,chosen,selected
→ USA
→ chairman,president
→ November (Heshvan)
HC 5776=AD 2015-2016,YEARS 2015-2016=HC 5776,AD 2015-2016=HC 5776

DJTrump, USA, president, November (Hebrew month 'Heshvan').

DJTrump   Novemba (Heshvan)

USA

←president

Matrix #2 has: 'DJTrump, USA, president, November (Hebrew
month 'Heshvan'). Key here is found encoded from Exodus 36:20 to
Deuteronomy 1:28, by skipping 5963 letters.

Fig. 19

Key   'tenismach'
→ Meraiah , MARIAH, MARIA
→ Shara-
→ -pova   "Ten(n)isMa(t)ch, Maria, Shara-pova, Rus, Fr(e)nch, HC5760 (1999-2000)."
→ Fr(e)nch
→ Rus
→ YEARS 1999-2000=HC 5760,

Matrix 1 of 1 found of Key, from Numbers 16:15 to 26:7. Skip 764 letters
to find Key encoded. Odds are 1 in 500,000.

Part B → (below)

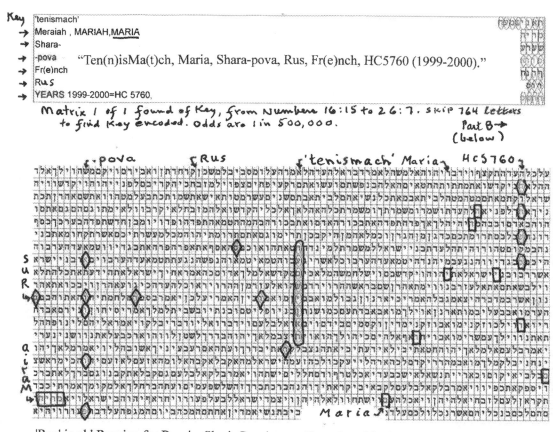

'Rus' is old Russian for Russia. She is Russian, and has played in the French pen tennis
match as a professional. She is also Christian, and wears a cross around her neck – please
note left of the Key the perfect <u>cross</u> shape formed by vertical '-pova' and horizontal 'Rus.'

Fig. 20

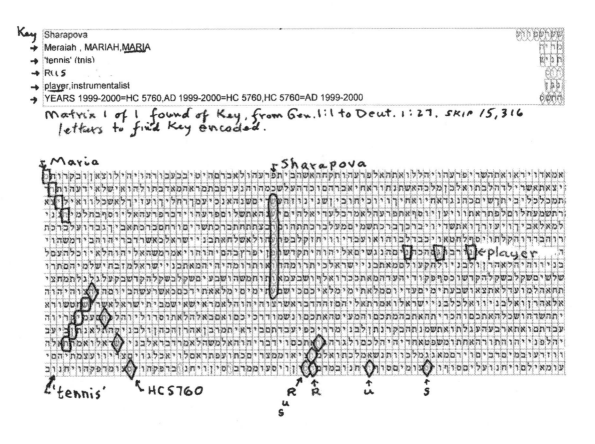

"Sharapova, Maria, tennis, player, Rus, HC5760 (1999-2000)."
'Tennis' is phonetic, and Rus is old Russian for Russia. The Hebrew Calendar year 5760 (1999-2000) is one of the years she played professional tennis.

Fig. 21

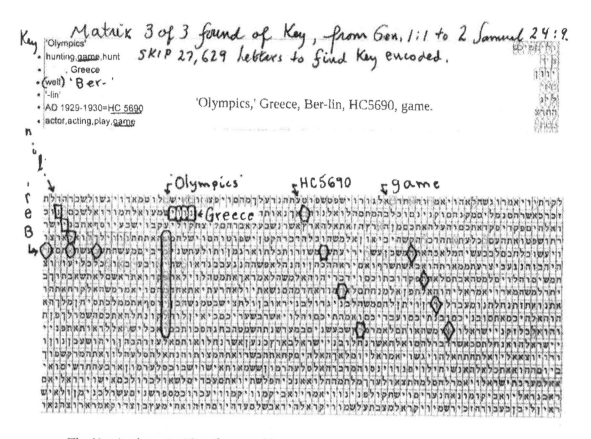

'Olympics,' Greece, Ber-lin, HC5690, game.

The Key is phonetic. The Olympics began in Greece as a set of sports games. In 1936 the Berlin Olympics were held. The Hebrew Calendar year HC5690 lies within the calendar adjustment range needed to correct our Gregorian Calendar (see Appendix).

The whole history of the Olympics could be found encoded, comprising a large book which would include the encoded names of all participating countries, location, both summer and winter, and all the sports, all the participants, and all the winners of gold, silver, and bronze medals in all events.

Fig. 22

Key: cropc(i)rcl(e)
→ UFO
→ Olam   "CropCircle (phonetic), UFO, Olam (biblical name for Nibiru, per Sitchin),
→ N(i)b(i)ru   N(i)b(i)ru" (solar system's 10the planet, home of the Anunnaki, ancient astro-
→ Anun-   nauts who colonized Earth and created humans as a genetic hybrid; see Sitchin).
→ -aki

Matrix 1 of 1 found of Key, from 2 Samuel 18:18 to 2 Chronicles 36:23.
All books of the Tanach searched.

- Part A -

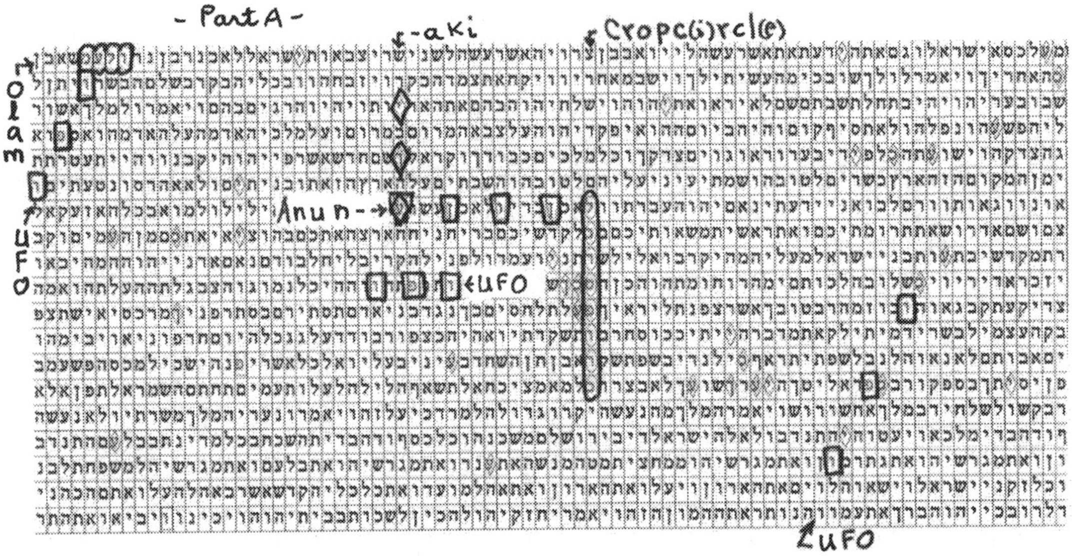

- Part B -

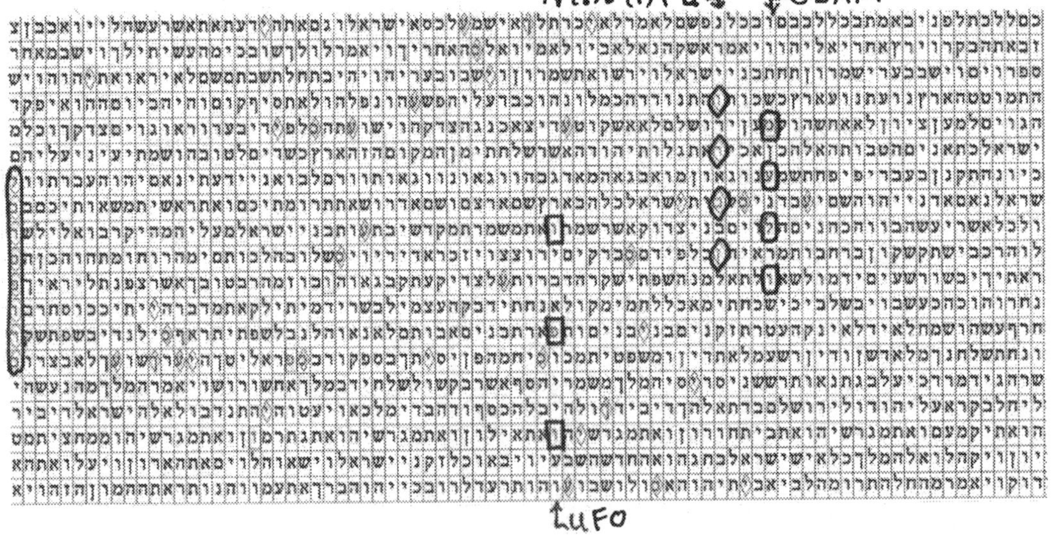

Fig. 23

"OlamUFOs, crop, circle, N(i)b(i)ru, Anu-naki."
Crop circles are made by UFO craft from Olam,
biblical name for Nibiru, 10th planet of the solar system,
(see Sitchin's books of his *Earth Chronicle* series) home
of the Anunnaki (see Sitchin).

Matrix 1 of 1 found of Key, from Gen. 6:22 to Leviticus 15:5.
skip 7891 letters to find Key encoded.

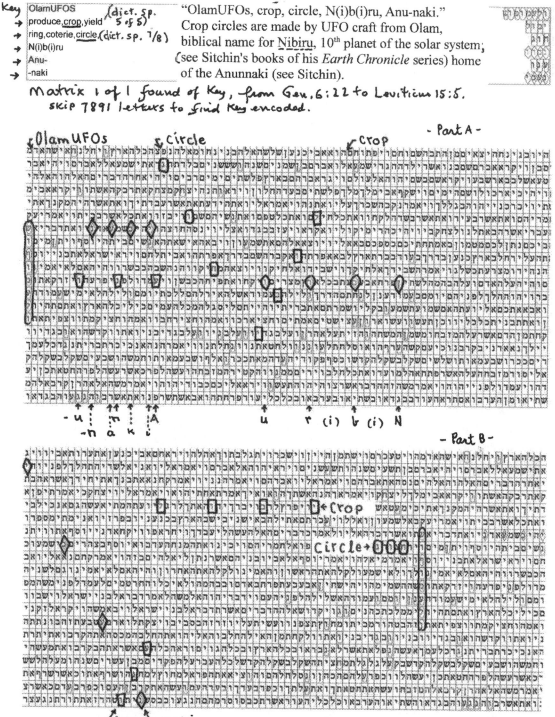

- Part A -

OlamUFOs   circle   crop

- Part B -

Anu- -naki

BOOK 4

CROP CIRCLES' ANCIENT SYMBOLIC CODE

Interpretation of Ancient Sumerian Symbols Used in Crop Circles in
Southern England Reveal Identity and Origin of the Circle Makers

My first website, *Crop Circle Books.com*, built and put online by Trish my web mistress in about the year 2000, was taken down against my wishes by way of the host, *Vivid*, going out of business and the billing cycle getting messed up at the end of their business existence, in about 2010. It was taken over by another company, but too late to revive or retrieve the digital content of the website. I reproduce the text of the website here as best I can. The site had graphics of photos of the 40 or so books that are not reproduced here. Prices listed here are for only historical record purposes, listed as they were on the original website and do not apply today as some of the books are no longer available. If the reader is interested in any particular title and cannot find it for sale on Amazon or elsewhere, I can be contacted at my residence at 1123 N. Las Posas, Ridgecrest, CA 93555 for current availability and price. If the reader finds some of my early booklets listed on the internet by re-sellers or collectors for extraordinary prices in the hundreds of dollars (yes, they are out there for those sale amounts!), please contact the author for the title(s) at 50% reduced price, and free shipping. When I produce my own volumes, there is no such thing as 'out of print,' no matter what other people claim.

Crop Circle Books Welcome to my website. There are new updates on latest discoveries and new title added in 2005. Major breakthrough to Egyptian Gods connection to crop circles and 'resurrection' of Osiris through tetrahedrally mediated elevations measured from Stonehenge and the Mars Face point to interdimensional return of the circle makers, the Anunnaki from Nibiru.

Another level of analysis, Anunnaki names searched for and found encoded in the Torah (the Five Books of Moses), reveals return to Babylon and Uruk in southern Iraq (ancient Sumeria) by about 2020 (according to the corrected Gregorian Calendar) by the Anunnaki. Calendar scholars have shown that the Gregorian Calendar is too low in its count of years since the birth of Jesus by between, 4 and 9 years.

See my second website, *Bible Crop Circle Codes*.com.

28 books are offered here, all written by Steve Canada, on crop circles, UFOs, Mars structures, the returning goddess, the Anunnaki, and the ancient Egyptian gods. He is the author

of *Crop Circle Language* (newly reintroduced series in 2003; vols.1-6 available), has developed an internationally reviewed theory (England, Germany, Italy) that deciphers new information presented in crop circle designs each season. He was a consultant for and was interviewed by Fox TV's "Encounters" series in 1994.

Crop Circle Meanings – Understanding the Symbols

I have discovered the key to deciphering the redundant, repetitive patterns in Crop Circles. They are a communication system. Linear, multi-symbol crop formations are decipherable as statements. Other of my published books through Author House fully explain and illustrate this, so that essential information will not be repeated here.

Mandala crop circle designs over the decades have identified all 12 names on the Anunnaki Ruling Council of 12; see Sitchin, and Book #110.

Using clearly identifiable symbols (Sumerian in origin), the circle makers have identified the planet of their origin, who they are, some of their ancient and on-going programs of interest (such as genetics-reproduction) and possibly an indication of what we can expect when they return to Earth ('Eridu,' their 'Home in the Faraway').

Their return is encoded in the Torah. My book *Bible Crop Circle Codes* shows this. Others of my books show all 12 Anunnaki names encoded with all gods of all religions in all of human history.

If music is the universal language, then I have discovered a new level of message encoded in the sky on crop circle creation dates. A one hundred percent match found in elevation angle ratios to ancient Egyptian gods (in the sky as stars) measured from Stonehenge and the Mars Face (ground level) at tetrahedral moments – see book #s106, 112, 121, and *Crop Circles 2002*.

Steve Canada, "who reads the signs in heaven and on Earth." (Michael Hesemann, March 5, 2001, Laughlin, Nevada, at UFO Conference; a major European UFO and crop circle researcher, a German journalist accredited to the Vatican, and author of *The Fatima Secret*.

"I'll never think of crop circles the same way again." Father Charlie Moore, Catholic priest, attorney, and scholar, April 29, 1995, Santa Cruz, Calif., after our panel presentation together.

Book #100: Crop Circle Meanings – Understanding the Symbols: The Returning Goddess and Coming Transformations

While this book is not as heavily illustrated as most of the others, it does present a cogent form of the theme of the goddess Inanna, the Sumerian goddess of grain (is it any wonder then that we see her messages in fields of cultivated grain?) as depicted in many crop formation designs. Later, in Mesopotamia, she was *Ishtar*, and later, in Egypt, *Asta (Isis,* in Greek) – see the author's book "Crop Circles and the Mistresses of the Martian Pyramids," and "Inanna book series." Some of the chapter-essays included in this book are: Transformation; A Decoding Key; New World Order; and the

Mandelbrot; Kultur and Civilization – a Dialectic History; Form and Function – Deconstruction; Love and Irony – Alpha and Omega; Information Technology – Understanding the Crop Circles' Symbols Regarding signal analysis. In the "Nexus" chapter the author also explains the origin of two other modern mysteries – the Mars Cydonia structures, and UFO craft. He uses evidence tied to crop circles – shared mathematical constants, per Richard Hoag-land's invaluable work; and observed craft and lights seen, videotaped, and photographed in the day and at night, in and near crop formations. Using this evidence, the author builds three syllogisms that show clear logic of his uncluttered explanations. In most of his books, because of the vast implications of his findings and conclusions, this "Nexus" chapter is included. If the reader is interested in learning more of how these three mysteries are related and the author's theory that explains their origin, order the 1993 book (updated in 1996) "Crop Cicles, UFOs, and Mars Structures – Their Common Origin."

ISBN 1883424-372 1995; expanded 2002 ed., 150pp., 8"x7" $9.95

Book #101: **Crop Circles – A Convergence of Narrative: Making Sense of the Symbols, Closing the Loop of History. Answering the Question, "Why in England?"**

Ancient history is revealed through the contemporary phenomenon of crop field designs. The convergence of referring to old stories in the historical record, within the framework of the modern era, is the telling sign of an emerging urgency at communication with humanity from beyond Earth. We are witnessing an energetic commitment on the part of the circlemakers to make clear to us in a redundant system of comprehensive and specific references exactly the nature of the forces and intention behind this notification effort of crop field formations. A universal story is being told through a variety of metaphors and images –process itself contained in static formations fashioned in bent crop stalks. Why in England? The meaning of the word 'British' gives us a major clue – 'Brit' comes from a root meaning 'New Covenant,' and '-ish' mans 'people of the.' And 'England' comes from the German of 'Engl' ('angel') and '-land' – so it is the Land of the Angel where those from Nibiru make their crop circle communication artifacts. Another clue is that while Z. Sitchin shows who designed and built Stonehenge (a people needing an astronomical data base of hundreds of thousands of years and the record-keeping and advanced mathematics to utilize and apply to such a precise time-keeping project), I have identified those same beings as specifically referred to and named individually in the English crop circles.

ISBN 1883424-402 1996 117pp., 8"x7" $7.95

#103: **Crop Circles – Mission Colony Earth**

Returning Colonizers From Ancient Astronauts' Planet Nibiru.
Will Rule be Reimposed? Will War be Waged?

This book focuses on the theme of colony and the first mission those explorers from Nibiru were on to Earth – in search for gold so they could bring it back to their home planet Nibiru, and suspend particles of gold in the atmosphere as some sort of protective shield (Ecological? Climatic? Preserve heat?). The saga of this first mission, about 450,000 years ago (see Sitchin) and subsequent ones, is told in the ancient Sumerian record. Included in this record is an accounting of the creation of species homo sapien by those from Nibiru, through genetic intervention and introduction of their own seed into a more primitive animal (see Sitchin's series of books).The Sumerians formed the fist recognizably modern civilization about 6000 years ago, and formulated systematic writing and record keeping. They told that the beings who taught them these things were from the tenth planet of the solar (see NASA 1987 press release announcing indirect detection of such a planet), taught them, ruled them, and led them in battle. Key questions addressed in this book are whether or not their rule will again be imposed, and if so, where, and on what scale? Given the long legacy of their ancient, warlike campaigns, will those from Nibiru specifically identified in crop formations again wage war, again sacrifice human armies in their conflicts among themselves for power and control?

ISBN 1883424-526 1998 120pp., 8"x7" $8.95

#104: **Crop Circles – The End of Time**

The Return to Earth of Allah, Quetzalcoatl, Ra, Vishnu, and Yahweh

Crop circles are a communication system (one which has been deciphered by the author) used by those returning from the 10th planet of the solar system (known as Nibiru in ancient texts) – see copy of the two 1987 NASA press releases in this book announcing the detection of a 10th planet of the solar system – to warn us of the coming end of historical time. Not the "end of the world," but the beginning of a new calendar. There is a reason why the Jewish calendar counts the current year at about 5770, and it has to do with those who are responsible for the crop circles. This "crop circle language" (the title of the author's first 10-volume series of booklets) is being demonstrated by those ancient visitors, teachers and rulers who began historical time, those who taught and ruled Sumeria 6000 years ago, those who (in Tep Zepi, i.e., "The First Time") built the Giza pyramids, those who built Stonehenge, … those returning to Earth.

ISBN 1883424-631 1996; 2nd ed., 2000; 114pp., 8"x7" $7.95

#105: **Crop Circles and the Mistresses of the Martian Pyramids**

England's Crop Circle Connection to Egypt's Giza Plateau and the Mars Cydonia Region

The Great Pyramid at Giza was known about in Sumeria and Mesopotamia. It was, along with the Sphinx, depicted in various texts there. Ninharsag ("Lady of Life") was the first Mistress of the Pyramid. She was also revered in Egypt as a goddess, and was called Hat-Hor. She was also the Mistress of the Sinai peninsula – a region that still retains the name of who ruled it, Nannar/Sin, who was the father of Inanna, who, as Isis, became the second Mistress of the Pyramid (see Sitchin). It has been shown that the layout of the Mars Cydonai structures fits perfectly the layout of the ancient monuments of south-central England, precisely in the region where most crop circles appear each year (see Richard Hoagland). The spiral (goddess symbol) that inscribes the Giza plateau (clockwise) is matched not only by huge clockwise spiral crop formations across the road from Stonehenge, but by the spiral the author discovered that connects the Mars Cydonia City center, counterclockwise outward to nearby pyramids and ending at the Face (the Martian Sphinx, as one Russian researcher called it).

ISBN 1883424-623 2nd edition, 2000; 8"x7" 104pp, $7.95

#106: **Crop Circles 2000** – Anunnaki and Ancient Egyptian Gods Again Inform Us of Their Pending Return

Viewed from Stonehenge on crop circle creation dates (using the *Redshift* astronomical program), the solution to the origin of at least three mysteries can be solved (UFOs, crop circles, and the Mars structures; synthesized by the author in 1993), and is even further strengthened by the tetrahedral geometry-related elevation angles of key Egyptian Gods' stars and planets, such as Sirius, Orion, Mars, Venus, and the sun. Moving far beyond his successful 10 years of identifying by name the ruling council pantheon members from Nibiru as the crop circle makers (while including the deciphering method in this book) he now confirms their ancient Egyptian Gods identities and relates the inter-dimensional resurrection theme of these findings to the "descent and return" theme of the Sumerian rulers (those from Nibiru) identified in the crop circles. Since these ancient rulers from the solar system's planet Nibiru were later Egyptian "Gods," there is no conflict between what the crop circles are telling us in their specific designs and the precise position of Egyptian Gods sky symbols on crop circle creation dates (with their 100% exact match to the set of angles, some of which come out of the "Message of Cydonia, Mars" – see R. Hoagland). It was so nice of John Sayer, editor of *The Cereologist*, in the summer 1998 edition of that publication in England to say of me: "... he must be the most prolific writer on crop circles."

ISBN 1883424-615 2003 expanded, revised ed., 8.5"x11" 420pp., $29.95

#107: **Crop Circles and Isis, "Mistress of the Great Pyramid" at Giza**

Crop circles point us to the most ancient beginnings, to what the Egyptians calledTep Zepi (approx.: "First Time"). While at this point we might only have a crop circle and Giza pyramid connection by way of Ishtar/Inanna, the "Mistress of the Pyramid" being clearly identified in various ways throughout years of crop formations, this connection is enough to at least alert us to a need to acquaint ourselves with the established laws, wisdom, symbols and rituals practiced and used by the gods of the First Time. While renewal is a major theme of crop formations (such as the Mandel- brot formations near Cambridge denoting transformation in the chaos theory transition function), the annual cycle of the circles with Isis (i.e., Inanna) so intimately involved, would suggest to us reference back to the early Pyramid Age, from which an idea of such rebirth came. While in Egypt this took a star-monument form (pyramid shafts point to stars of the First Time), we can look today to the agri-symbol language of the circle makers for their rebirth (and return) message. The Sumerian goddess of grain, Inanna, was known in Egypt as *Asta* (*Isis* in Greek). Inanna replaced Ninharsag (the first Mistress of the Great Pyramid) on the Council of 12 of the Anunnaki ("From Heaven Those Who Came Down to Earth" -- see Sitchin).

ISBN 1883424-496 92pp., 8"x7" $6.95

#108: **Crop Circles, UFOs, and Music**

An American astronomer famous for decoding some mathematics of the Great Pyramid at Giza, compared the diameter measurements of some crop formations and found one ratio that stood out. It formed the diatonic scale of music – notes played by the white keys on a piano. Witnesses to a late-night UFO craft above a field heard a series of perfect-pitch musical notes. One of the witnesses was a musician who later transcribed the notes. The full report of this UFO encounter is included in this book. The author analyzed these notes and found a remarkable match to an ancient ratio, one connected to those responsible for presenting to us the communication system of crop circles.

ISBN 1883424-339 1994, 100pp., 8"x7" $8.95

#109: **Crop Circles – The Theory That Works**

Their Meaning for Mankind and Implications for History

The author has discovered that crop circles identify, using ancient Sumerian symbols, who are responsible for the genuine crop formations and where these makers are from. If the interpretation of the circles and their specific references is accurate, then it would seem that these ancient astronaut colonizers, teachers, leaders and rulers are returning to Earth.

In this book are presented three original deciphering methods developed over the years – developed as the circles have developed, have multiplied, proliferated, gotten larger and more complex over the decades, that is, since the first simple circles were documented in the summer of 1976 (not a coincidence the author claims, given what was occurring at Mars at the same time, that is, NASA photos being taken of the Cydonia region, revealing complex and huge, artificial structures). In Cydonia. Mathematical constants were later discovered to be shared by Cydonia geometry and crop formation designs, discovered by R. Hoagland; see his book, "The Monuments of Mars." Essentially the author allows the evidence, historical record, and facts to speak for themselves. If a crop formation's design transformational graphic dynamic (an awkward term, to be sure, but one fully described and examined in detail as applied to the large, 300-feet long Alton Barnes formation in question) parallels precisely all the extant verses of the oldest example of human writing, a Sumerian poem about the 7-step disrobing of the Sumerian goddess of grain (!) Inanna, then so be it. No 'belief' is needed to see the careful matching the author presents, connecting each design element with a particular poem verse. The long-standing and consistent successful matching of crop formation design elements (whether it be ancient symbols, or counting these elements, or the above transformational aspects) with ancient Sumerian knowledge is the key breakthrough the author presents as the beginning of a process to welcome those from Nibiru to Earth.

ISBN 1883424-534 1997 125pp., 8.5"x11" $9.95

#110: **Crop Circles – How to Read the Mandala Formations**

The power of my crop circle interpretation theory is demonstrated by the fact that the annual presentation of crop circle designs are consistent within the context of the Sumerian culture symbol set which deals with those who ruled them and where these advanced people were from. I discovered this extraordinary match in 1990 and it has been strengthened and verified in the interim years of each crop circle season, and reflected over the decades of the mysterious phenomenon. The congruence has held from the beginning of the crop circle seasons (first documented in 1976; no coincidence, I contend, given our activities in Mars orbit that very same summer). I predict this congruence will continue to hold true to that body of knowledge and understanding of those early visitors to Earth, those rulers from Nibiru. After I first wrote and published this book, in 1997, I found the quote below and added it to page 30 of the revise edition: "In Sanskrit the word 'Mandala' literally means circle and center … At the center of the Mandala is the abode of the Deity" (Haddington, p.172). I felt vindicated that I had discovered one of my decipherment methods without the benefit of this Sanskrit Mandala principle. In this book is revealed a method of counting circle design elements and thus identifying the particular Anunnaki named on the Council of 12 by their rank-order number. All 12 names are revealed in the crop circles by using this method.

ISBN 1883424-593 1997; 2ⁿᵈ ed. 2000; 90pp, 4"x6" $4.95

#111: **Crop Circles – A Vocabulary of the Symbols**

This book, 175 pages long and 8"x5" is a good digest, reference and overview of my theory through 1998. I wrote no book in 1999 (retired early and moved to the desert). In Appendix 1, on p.151, there is "A Taxonomy of Some Crop Circle Types," cross-referenced with chapters in the book – types such as Plain Circle (Nibiru), Ringed Circle (Nibiru), Crosses (Nibiru), Six-Pointed Star (Mars), Forked Lightning (Marduk's Weapon), Scorpion ('Bull of Heaven' weapon), Spiral (Goddess), Key (mining), Triangle (fertility, thus reproduction, genetics), and Mandalas (count of their design elements matches rank number on the Anunnaki Ruling Council, as listed in Sumeria, per Sitchin).

If this frenetic display of such diverse designs in the crop fields of England does not comprise a "vocabulary of the symbols" (each deciphered by the author using references to researchable ancient texts), what would? This seminal compilation book includes excerpts from eight of my previous crop circle interpretation books.

ISBN 1883424-542 1998 158pp, 8"x7" $9.95

#112: **Crop Circles 1999 – Dancing with Egyptian Stars at Stonehenge**

Star Alignments Viewed From Stonehenge Show Return of Ancient Egyptian Pantheon

Viewed from Stonehenge on crop circle creation dates, the solution to the origin of three mysteries (UFOs, crop circles, and the Mars structures: synthesized by the author in 1993) is further strengthened by the tetrahedral geometry-related elevation angles of the key Egyptian Gods' stars and planets, such as Sirius, Orion, Mars, Venus and the sun. Moving far beyond his successful 10 years of identifying by name the Nibiru ruling council-pantheon members as the crop circle makers (while including his deciphering methods in this book) he now confirms their ancient Egyptian Gods identities and relates the interdimensional resurrection theme of these findings to the "descent and return" theme of the Sumerian rulers (those from Nibiru) identified in the crop circles.

ISBN 1883424-64x 3-bk series combined in 2000; expanded in 2003; 8"x11" 416pp., $29.95

#113: Crop Circles, UFOs, and Mars Structures – Their Common Origin

Evidence of 3 Separate but Related Mysteries Ties Them Together in a Logical Way

This book is also titled with "UFOs" as the first word of the title; … no matter, be assured that it is the same book. Summarized in extremely condensed form as 'Nexus' chapter in many other titles by the author, this book is a good example of the synthesis process of theory-building, not as academic abstraction but as applied to evidence from disparate sources derived from researchers in three different areas of interest, namely: (1) my crop circle deciphering methods (yielding what they refer to as design constructions); (2) UFO craft evidence as it relates to crop circles (eyewitness accounts, photographs, and videos of various objects and lights in and near formations, in the day and night); and (3) mathematical constants shared by the Mars Cydonia structures and crop formations (as discovered by Richard Hoagland; see his book 'The Monuments of Mars"). Using these sets of evidence and findings I build three airtight syllogisms that show the clear logic of this uncluttered explanation for the common origin of these three modern mysteries. In most of my books, because of the vast implications of my findings and conclusions I wish to share with the world, the highly condensed *Nexus* chapter is included, usually as an Appendix. This book is basically composed of the complete texts of 3 previous books: 'UFO's Origin Identified,' 'Crop Circles and Mars,' and 'The Mars Structures – Who Made Them?'

ISBN 1883424-240 8"x7" 180pp., $12.95

#114: Crop Circles and the Returning Rulers From the Biblical Planet Olam

Three original, distinct decipherment methodologies inform the phenomenology of this crop circle design analysis. While the method is partly deconstructionist in its approach, it adheres to the wholistic integrity of what is presented (its heart open to the sky, inscribing upon the waiting earth) in the fertile crop fields of England. With a new Introduction and Afterword, this book includes excerpts from seven of my previous 48 crop circle deciphering books:

Crop Circles: A Vocabulary of the Symbols.
Crop Circles and the Tree of Life.
Crop Circles – Allah's Daughter Returns to Earth.
Crop Circles and Isis.
Crop Circles – A Convergence of Narrative.
Crop Circles and the Mistresses of the Martian Pyramids.
Crop Circles: The End of Time.

For those who doubt the alien origin of genuine crop circles, I have these questions: How do you explain chromosomal abnormalities, depleted soil moisture, the swollen bending-point nodules, the unbroken plant stalks, radiation residues, dust and pesticide residue left undisturbed on laid-down plants, the weaving of plant stalks (some-times two layers in opposite directions) of the grain? If anyone can explain these using conventional means, that person would be doing us all a favor. The British government is very concerned about "an unknown force entering its national territory" (Queen Elizabeth's terminology) at will and laying down strange inscriptions on private property and in the public's food supply. The British army has tried unsuccessfully to reproduce crop circles with what are considered genuine properties. There is an intensive effort in Britain to discredit and discount crop circles as a genuine mystery worthy of serious public concern. The website "cropcirclemakers.com" (avowed crop circle hoaxers claiming credit) has on it a banner requesting interested persons to apply to MI-5, the British Intelligence Service. Can they be more blatant?

ISBN 1883424-550 8"x7" 180pp., $12.95

#115: Crop Circles – Allah's Daughter Returns to Earth

Before Inanna was known by this name (literally "Anu's Beloved") she was *Irninni*. After sleeping with her great-grandfather, Anu (also known as An, head ruler of planet Nibiru) in the city of Uruk, on one of his rare visits to Earth (the Hebrew calendar was started on the occasion of one of these visits; see Z. Sitchin) she was renamed *Inanna* (see Sitchin, 1996, pp.166-167). Inanna/Ishtar was the daughter of Nannar/Sin (a member of the Nibiru ruling council of 12), who Sitchin (1996, p.363) has identified as later becoming known as Allah, the God of Islam. Inanna has been repeatedly identified in the crop circles over the decades, and with the Return theme (by way of 'descent') depicted in the field designs, we can infer that her return to Earth might be imminent.

ISBN 1883424-518 8"x7" 150pp, $9.95

#116: Crop Circles and National Security

In this volume the prior editions of a series of 'National Security' booklets are combined between two covers. An unknown force is entering at will and with impunity the national territory of Britain, creating large and numerous crop formations on a seasonal basis. The British army has tried to stop the craft making them, using helicopters to maneuver and interfere, but without success. Since the primary duty of any central government is protection of the borders and national integrity, the implications for nationals security have not escaped those authorities responsible for carrying out their defense mandate. While a well-funded misinformation effort has been underway for some time, it will be to no avail once these government bureaucrats realize who they will have to deal with – the real circle makers. What is called "coercive diplomacy" (informative announcements, coupled with veiled threats) is contained in these "diplomatic cables" we call crop circles. Ancient Anunnaki weapons have been portrayed in some crop formations – see Book #124.

ISBN 1883424-674 1993, 6-bk series combined in 2001, 8"x7" 250pp, $18.95

#117: **Crop Circle Origins**

Ancient Symbols Used Reveal Where Circlemakers Are From

Who are making the crop circles, and why? Where are they from? What does the pictogrammic, symbolic information system mean? Is it a communication system? These questions are answered in this book, using documented, ancient evidence. Much more is also explained in this ground-breaking work, which uses ancient texts of the written human historical record to decipher specific symbols that are repeatedly and carefully crafted into these "crop circle" designs, which turn out to be, upon examination, comparison and analysis, communication artifacts.

ISBN 1883424-100 2002 expanded edition; 8.5"x7" 70pp., $4.95

#118: **Crop Circles and Genetics**

Reproduction, Bioengineering, and Immortality

The message of transformation so clearly depicted in the crop formations is also perceived in the chromosomal changes found by Dr. Levengood in seeds taken from bent plant stalks within crop circles. These seeds, when replanted, have higher than usual yields – an interesting possible "message" in itself. The focus on genetics of the abduction-inter-breeding taking place worldwide in the UFO-alien-human abduction scenario (each one scripted with the exact same sequence of steps) is a corroborating phenomenon which might shed light on the suggested descriptive depictions in the fields of reproduction (sperm, and female reproductive system) and of the DNA genetic code itself portrayed in formations and in the stuff of life itself, i.e., genetically engineered agricultural crop seed strains. The gene that determines when cells live or die has been discovered (*Science News* article shown in this book). The fact that we are getting closer to controlling our own life spans puts us again in danger of being "expelled from the garden" by those who first established the E.DIN (see Sitchin). The "Tree of Life" metaphor for knowledge contained in the secrets of physical immortality, is the preserve of those long-ago visitors who developed that knowledge and who apply the genetics of eternity to only themselves.

ISBN 1883424-070 8.5"x7" 88pp, $6.95.

119: **RA and the Vatican: Crop Circles and the Return of RA,**

The Egyptian Sun God, Lord of Time

The subtitle of this book is: "On Crop Circle Creation Dates in 1999, 2000 and 2001 the Rising Sun Heralds the Resurrection of RA. The Timing, Seen from Stonehenge, is Mediated by Tetrahedrally positioned Osiris (Orion) and Isis (Sirius). The Anunnaki-Created Crop Circles Announced the Return of Those Sumeria Rulers from Nibiru, Later Known as the Egyptian Pantheon."

Excerpts from three prior books analyzing the English crop circles of 1999, 2000, and 2001 – after identifying the Anunnaki crop circles maker named in each deciphered formation, selecting out those moments on crop circle creation dates when either Orion is positioned (using *Redshift* astronomy program) at -19.5 degrees or on the horizon (the ancient Egyptian 'Rebirth' position), or the star Sirius is -33 degrees – and noting that the sun (RA) is rising only at these moments. At these clock times some other Pantheon members' elevation angles are also noted, and these are compared to a set of seven key angles on Earth and at Cydonia, Mars – the nearly 100% match between these two sets of angles is noted and discussed as a highly significant aspect of the Anunnaki communication artifacts we call Crop Circles.

ISBN 1883424-747 July 2002 edition; 8.5"x11"; 318 pp, $29.95

#120 **Crop Circles – Interplanetary Communication Begins**

Four volumes of my "Communication Book Series" combined between tow covers:
Volume 1: Crop Circles as Communication Artifacts
Volume 2: Crop Circles as Interplanetary Communication
Volume 3: Crop Circles – Media, Metaphor, Meaning
Volume 4: Crop Circles – Decrypting, Deciphering, Decoding – "The Medium is the Message" (Marshall McLuhan, 1964).

These volumes contain essays on such subjects as the nature of media, cultural interface, signal, noise-background, entropy-redundancy ratio yielding message, brain hemispheres and perception, word-metaphor structure, impact on society of artifacts, etc...

ISBN 1883424-666 2nd edition 2001, 134 pp., 8"x7" $9.95

#121 **Crop Circles 2001 – Anunnaki from Nibiru Continue Naming**

Themselves. Egyptian Gods' Interdimensional Return

See description of Book #106, "Crop Circles 2000 – Anunnaki and Ancient Egyptian Gods." Basically the same findings but from different crop circle formations and on different dates during the summer of 2000.

ISBN 1883424-682 revised ed., 2003, 383pp, 8.5"x11" $29.95

#122 **Crop Circles and Goddess Inanna, Queen of Heaven and Earth**

What the genuine crop designs refer to are ancient texts of Sumeria, Mesopotamia and Akkadia in which are recorded symbols for what these people were taught by their leaders and rulers from the 10th planet of the solar system, Nibiru ("Planet of Crossing" – see various crosses as a crop circle type). In 1987 NASA reported indirect detection of a 10th solar system planet. The press release is presented in this book. Repeatedly and consistently the circles lead us to the goddess. The language of the circles (shown by the author to be such a communication system, in such books as book #120), among other things, helps us understand some important aspects of our past perhaps forgotten. It seems clear at this point that the Sumerian "Goddess of Grain" (no longer any need to wonder why this communication is in fields of grain!), Inanna, is notifying us of her identity, presence, and her impending return to Earth. The metaphor of hope is unmistakable … for renewal, rebirth, regeneration, return.

ISBN 1883424-658 6-bk series combined in 2001; 8"x7" 390pp., $29.95

Fig. 24

Inanna's descent depicted graphically.
This 300-feet-long crop formation of July 11,
1990 at Alton Barnes, Wiltshire states:
"Inanna descends (with) Nibiru's multiplied
'Marduk's Lightning Weapon'"

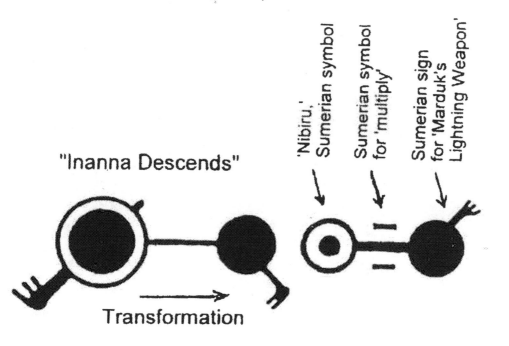

"Inanna Descends"

Transformation

'Nibiru,'
Sumerian symbol

Sumerian symbol
for 'multiply'

Sumerian sign
for 'Marduk's
Lightning Weapon'

Transformation depicts disrobement of Inanna at 6
gates upon visiting her rival sister in southern Africa
to learn mining. Note more complex design on left
side. Detailed explanation of step-by-step transformation of "Inanna's Descent" (this Sumerian saga
is the oldest example of human writing, in Sumerian
cuneiform) is shown in most of the author's other
books; see Joseph Campbell reference.
Inanna is required to remove her crown (head band),
staff, jewels, ring, and breastplate. Note that graphic,
crop inscribed representative depictions of these
present on the left side have been 'removed' (not all
design elements are shown here), resulting in the
simpler design on the right.

#123 **Crop Circles and the Tree of Life**

The Earth is Dying – The Eden Gods are Returning

Arcturus Books editor said: "One would do well to consider the thoughts contained in this work." This book explores the two main interpretations of the Tree of Life: first, as the genetic code of all living things; second, as the "forbidden" Tree of Life in the Garden/Orchard of Eden, which apparently held the secret to immortality (an ability attained by those interplanetary explorers who established the E.DIN, per Z. Sitchin), the knowledge about which was to be denied humans. The human threat to all life on Earth is evident through research done worldwide. The destructive effects of industrial societies are being felt at an accelerating pace. Effects on some local ecologies have been devastating. Given that the planetary system has an inter-dependent, feedback, operational threshold which cannot be crossed without breakdowns with cascading effects throughout the system, and since we do not know where that general threshold is, our insistence on polluting more (a reflection of population explosion pressure on the environment and growing consumer demand) is done in violation of a stewardship bestowed upon us millennia ago. The recent speed-up in planet-wide extinctions of plant and animal species puts us closer to facing our own extinction. J. Schell, in his 1992 book, *The Fate of the Earth*, writes extensively on the nature of extinction and how discovering the deeper meaning of extinction helps to discover new meanings of human life.

ISBN 1883424-488 8"x7" 108pp., $7.95

#124 **Crop Circles 1994 – Interim Report and the Returning "Bull of Heaven"**

Author's translation theory reveals consistent findings with previous seasons. New decoding principles discovered, and new identities of returning rulers are uncovered. More Mars connections are illustrated. Implications of the Depiction of an ancient Anunnaki weapon, the 'Bull of Heaven,' are interpreted. A recurrent theme of this season is a reiteration of the 1990 season's, that of return – the return of Nibiru as it nears the region of the rest of the solar system's planets (from below at an angle of 30 degrees to the ecliptic and in a retrograde orbit, according to ancient records cited and described by Z. Sitchin in his popular books, starting in 1978 with *The 12th Planet*). Coupled with this theme of the planet's return is the message that the particular beings specifically identified are also returning. They ruled us before and they will rule us again. The planet Nibiru is on its way back to the region of the Asteroid Belt, its nearest point to the sun, its Place of Crossing, hence its literal name in Sumerian, "Planet of Crossing." In 1998 I noticed how many varieties of crosses were crop circle types, so I discovered their meaning as symbolically referring us to that ancient knowledge. One of the Sumerian symbols for Nibiru was a cross. The use of "The Bull of Heaven" weapon may not be a foregone conclusion, is we respond appropriately tot the crop circle notification system. The depiction of any weapon might be only a reminder and a warning of likely consequences if certain instructions or directives are not followed.

ISBN 1883424-380 2 books from 1995 combined in 2000; 8"x7" 200pp., $14.95

BOOK 5

TEN ALIEN MYSTERIES SOLVED – A DEEP WEB OF CODED MEANING UNCOVERED

First, center the argument in the arena of evidence anyone can find. Testing the supporting hypotheses with as direct sources as can be defended with documented history will guide us to the best possible explanation for the phenomenon we are trying to explain. Then build a theory based on these hypotheses.

The power of a theory is measured by how much it can explain, and how many different phenomena it can account for. My theory, built over 19 years of research and study, ties together UFOs, crop circles, the Mars structures, and the Torah (the Five Books of Moses in the original Hebrew text, about 3400 years old) as having **one** source, the Anunnaki of Nibiru, those ancient astronauts who came to Earth about half a million years ago in search for gold and who much later genetically created a 'primitive worker' (humans), to help them work in the mines and serve them in other ways too.

These Anachim of Olam (biblical name for Nibiru, per Sitchin), the 'Nephilim' ('Those Who Came Down;' not 'angels,' and not 'giants,' which was a mistaken translation, per Sitchin), are returning soon, as indicated in their crop circles (especially starting in August 1990 at Alton Barnes in England with a long, complex crop field design) and encoded in their dictated-to-Moses-text, the Torah.

Index List of Alien Mysteries Solved:

1   What Makes Crop Circles?
2   What Do Crop Circles Mean?
3   Where Do UFOs Come From?
4   Why the 'Descend' and 'Transformation' Theme of Crop Circles?
5   Who Are Responsible for UFOs?
6   Were All Major Civilizations Established by Ancient Astronauts?
7   Are All the Main Gods of All Major Religions Encoded in the Torah?
8   Who Was Yahweh, Lord of the Hebrews?
9   How and Why is Much of Human History Encoded in the Torah?
10 Who Made the Mars Structures at Cydonia, and Have They Returned?

Alien Mystery #1: What Makes Crop Circles?

Three bodies of evidence point to UFOs as responsible for creating crop circles –One: **videos** during the day showing small globes of light descending into fields before crop circles are formed, and after crop circles form; more than one example of this was shown worldwide on television, of a large field with a huge formation in it, with crowds of people on the raised roadbed along the field's perimeter. Two: Years of accumulated **eyewitness reports** reveal a variety of UFO types (including large disc craft seen in the daytime hovering over fields and 'shooting' beams of light down into the fields, after which complex crop-inscribed formations are discovered) associated in time and space with the appearance of crop circles.

Three: **still photos** have captured images of small discs on the ground in the center of some crop circles; see such a photo in Pat Delgado and Colin Andrews' book *Circular Evidence*.

Alien Mystery #2: What Do Crop Circles Mean?

Do their designs contain information we can use to understand their possible references or intent or purpose of their designs? Crop circles use ancient Sumerian symbols to identify Nibiru, tenth planet of the solar system, home planet of the Anunnaki – such as *large circle* (Sumerian symbol for the number 3600, the number of years for Nibiru's orbit around the sun), *ringed circle* (Sumerian symbol for Nibiru as a 'haloed' planet as seen from Earth, and *crosses* of various types ('Nibiru' means literally 'planet or place of crossing' at its nearest point to the sun, in the asteroid belt between Mars and Jupiter).

Crop circles identify by name the 12 members of the Anunnaki ('From Heaven Those Who Came Down to Earth'; the ancients called Nibiru 'Heaven') Ruling Council, as shown in my Book #110, *Crop Circles –How to Read the Mandala Formations*. The Sumerians recorded these 12 Anunnaki names as members of the Ruling Council, in rank-succession order from 60 down to 5 in intervals of 5; see Sitchin's book series *Earth Chronicles*.

Crop Circles also identify the circle makers' ongoing interest in their past projects, such as mining, and genetics-reproduction-interbreeding (see my book #118, *Crop Circles and* Genetics). Two weapons they used in ancient times while on Earth are depicted in crop circles – Marduk's 'Lightning Weapon,' and the 'Bull of Heaven' – as a reminder and warning (see book #116, *Crop Circles and National Security*; and book #124, *Crop Circles 1994 … the 'Bull of Heaven'*).

Alien Mystery #3: Where Do UFOs Come From?

A third of a century of consistent information derived from crop circles (which identify Nibiru and the Anunnaki by group and individual name by way of their rank on the Ruling Council as recorded by the Sumerians at least several thousand years ago) in their annual summer appearance in south-central England (a region of ancient monuments such as Stonehenge, Avebury, and Silbury Hill) leads to the logical conclusion that UFOs come from Nibiru, and that the returning Anunnaki are responsible for them. The logic of the best evidence is followed here in order to arrive at the strongest, most supportable conclusion. For related information, see my website www. AlienUFOCropCircles.com.

The 1962 abduction of Betty and Barney Hill is an example of missed-cues in communication. The alien leader aboard the saucer who asked Betty if she knew "where you are" on a chart she described as a "star map" put the chart away when she replied "no." Months or years after she drew what she recalled of the "map," and Marjorie Fish, a school teacher, interpreted it as a star chart revealing a double-star system as the origin of the saucer craft. Decades after that, two German researchers, Koch and Kyborg, re-analyzed Betty's diagram and found a perfect match for the solar system on the abduction date, all lines connecting to mineral-rich asteroids and planets, showing Jupiter used as a "gravity sling shot" and travel route of the saucer as coming from beyond the outer solar system. These findings are consistent with the Anunnaki as our neighbors whose long-standing interests lie in mining minerals and traveling to Earth.

Alien Mystery #4: Why the Crop Circle 'Descend' and 'Transformation' Theme?

The Anunnaki of Nibiru began the first human civilization, in Sumeria (present-day Iraq) about 5000 years ago. Z. Sitchin shows in his book series *Earth Chronicles* that the Anunnaki ('From Heaven Those Who Came Down to Earth') established every major culture in the world (see Mystery #7 below).

The **return** to this region and to other areas of the world by the Anunnaki, is foretold when the Torah is decoded as an 'Oracle' (see Mysteries #7 and #11 below). The specific "Descent of Inanna" (who was the ancient Sumerian Goddess of Grain) is depicted in the August 11, 1990 crop formation at Alton Barnes, Wiltshire (extensively photographed and even made famous by appearing on a music album cover).

See Fig. 24, on a previous page, for depiction of graphic.

The ancient Sumerian saga, *Descent of Inanna*, is the <u>oldest</u> example of human writing in existence. See Book #122, *Crop Circles and Goddess Inanna, Queen of Heaven and Earth*, in the text of by now defunct website 'Crop Circle Books.com.'

The several **'Mandelbrot'** crop configurations that have appeared carry the embedded message of 'transformation'; while popularly misinterpreted as denoting 'chaos,' actually the mathematical function describes 'transmutation' at the edge-interface of order-and-chaos ... the boundary holds within it the process of 'transmutation,' as *alchemy* refers to 'disorder' yielding 'order.' So the Anunnaki message here is they will bring **order** to a system on the edge of **'chaos'** ... as we see in the global economic and financial meltdown that started in 2008, along with mass migrations from war torn regions, and political changes such as the rise of nationalist movements.

Alien Mystery #5: Who Are Responsible for UFOs?

Since UFOs come from Nibiru (see Mystery #3 above), then the logical conclusion is that the **Anunnaki** from there are in charge of all UFO activities, programs, duties, tasks, assignments and functions. So everything that UFOs do are a result of decisions made by the Anunnaki, whether they be present only on Nibiru, or have returned to their base(s) on Mars (see Mystery #10 below, and my website www.MartianGods TorahEvidence.com), are on the far-side of the moon, or have undersea bases.

While the origin of the 'Greys' aboard UFO craft is an open question, the tall, Nordic type of humanoid 'alien' aboard such craft (who <u>might</u> be the Anunnaki themselves) have been reported to be in charge and have ordered the Greys around and even dismissed them at times, directing them in some of their duties.

The Grey-human inter-breeding program carried out aboard UFO craft (see books by Fowler, Jacobs, Strieber, and Hopkins) seems directed in only <u>one</u> direction, that of creating a hybrid species apparently to be integrated at an unknown rate into human society. Humans are <u>already</u>

a hybrid species, the result of genetic manipulation of an earthly primate female and sperm from an Anunnaki, as shown by Z. Sitchin starting with his 1978 book *The Twelfth Planet* and his later book *Genesis Revisited.*

So the Anunnaki creating <u>another</u> hybrid species to occupy Earth would not be out of character for them. Neither would <u>destroying</u> their creation (or at least trying to, as in the Deluge). Yahweh (who was the Anunnaki 'Enlil,' see Mysteries #7 and #8 below; and see Sitchin, *Divine Encounters*, 1996, Endpaper, pp.372-3, and pp.350-5) promised not to try to destroy humanity again – he will be able to keep his promise by merging human DNA with that of the Grey, and not destroy it. The results and implications of this are discussed below in Mystery #11,

Alien Mystery #6: Were All Major Civilizations Established by Ancient Astronauts?
Sitchin shows in his book series *Earth Chronicles* that the Anunnaki of Nibiru were responsible for developing the foundations of all ancient cultures, and even though pagan times attributed to them 'divine' qualities and named them as regional 'gods,' these human-like beings were from Nibiru and were our progenitors.

So the mystery of how ancient civilizations were founded and why all their 'gods' had attributes ascribed to various Anunnaki is solved through the explanation that Sitchin offers in his thoroughly researched history and original documents such as Sumerian cuneiform tablets – he was one of a handful of people who could read and translate them.

Insofar as religion is basic to civilizations, the thesis that the Anunnaki established all human cultures is supported and illustrated in my 9-volume book series *Aliens in World Religions*, described and featured and available on my website www.AliensInWorldReligions.com. This shows **all** gods of **all** religions throughout **all** of recorded human history are encoded in the Torah, *with* the 12 Anunnaki names in the Sumerian record of the Anunnaki Ruling Council. See also my 2-volume set *Bible Crop Circle Codes* that shows the 12 crop-circle-maker names, the Anunnaki, identified in crop circles *and* encoded, close together to each other, in the Torah; book featured at my website www.BibleCropCircleCodes.com.

Alien Mystery #7: Are All the Main Gods of All Major Religions Encoded in the Torah?
How is the Torah revealed as containing encoded within its text (dictated by Yahweh to Moses on top of Mt. Sinai over 40 days and nights about 3400 years ago, accord- ing to the Conservative Hebrew tradition) not only most if not all of human history but <u>all</u> the main 'gods' of <u>all</u> major religions throughout history, encoded in the text <u>with</u> the corresponding Anunnaki names?

How the Anunnaki encoded the Torah's text is a matter of speculation, but our conception goes to cryptology and advanced computers capable of such deep encryption. J. Santinover, in his 1998 book *Cracking the Bible Code*, points out that some NSA professional employees, after thoroughly investigating 'Bible Codes,' took early retirement and moved themselves and their families to Jerusalem to study and learn more.

Is there a connection between crop circles, UFOs, the Torah, and the 12 names on the Anunnaki Ruling Council? Yes, since 'OlamUFO' and 'cropcircl(e)' are encoded multiple times in the Torah, and <u>close together</u> in the same matrices. 'Olam' is the biblical name for 'Nibiru,' per Sitchin. 'Nibiru' is also encoded in the Torah, with various Anunnaki names. See my website <u>www. AnunnakiTorahBibleCodes.com</u>.

Alien Mystery #8: Who Was Yahweh, Lord God of the Hebrews?

Sitchin (*Divine Encounters*, 1996, Endpaper, pp.372-3, and pp.350-5) shows that Yahweh was the Anunnaki named *Enlil*, rank 50 on the Ruling Council as listed by the Sumerians. He is identified by this rank in various mandala-like crop circle designs, e.g. on August 25, 2008 at Eastfield, Alton Barnes, Wiltshire, among other crop formations over the decades in various field locations in south-central England.

Sitchin, in his 2004 book *The Earth Chronicles Expeditions*, shows where the <u>actual</u> Mt. Sinai is located; it's not where tourists are brought by Egyptian-sponsored tours. He shows his own personal photograph of a huge saucer on the ground on the real Mt. Sinai, where he had contracted to fly in the helicopter, but on approach the pilot turned around and refused to land.

The name of Enlil is encoded in the Torah with 'Yahweh,' so many times and so close together in some matrices it is difficult to convey the number and density. J. Santinover points out that such encoded proximity of terms is highly associated with things that are meaningfully related to each other, and is one of the hall marks of the Bible Code.

The more powerful a theory is, the more it explains. My theory not only explains who 'God' is, but also how communication (actually notification) from 'Heaven' (Nibiru) is being transmitted to humans via crop circles made by UFO craft – machines made on Nibiru and sent to Earth to carry out several missions critical to Anunnaki objectives.

Alien Mystery # 9: How and Why is Much of Human History Encoded in the Torah?

The assessment by encryption professionals is that we do not have the computing ability, even if *all* terminals and mainframes on the planet were linked, to do such extensive and deep encoding as found repeatedly and broadly in the Torah; see J. Satinover's 1996 book *Cracking the Bible Code*.

Rabbis about 900 years started to notice information buried in the Torah's text was retrievable if certain numbers of letters were skipped; their correspondence with each other over the centuries led to more developed and robust methodology that became known popularly as 'Bible Codes.'

So we do not know precisely *how* that text of 304,805 Hebrew letters was composed in such a way as to hold such vast numbers of encoded names, words and phrases so relevant to human history, such as the names of all main rabbis (along with their birth and death dates), important historical events such as assassinations (all of them over 4000 years, some even from before the Torah was composed and dictated) and attempts (Pope John II, *and* the name of the would-be killer), the sinking of the *Titanic*, and the 9-11 attack on the 'twin towers' in New York City. An exhaustive list would take too much space here; various resource books can guide the reader along this research avenue.

The *why* of it seems to point to a compact encyclopedia of human history that is' decode-able' by our computers starting in the 20th century. The timing of gaining such ability coincides with the time frame of 'signs' being presented indicating the return to Earth of those encryptors of the Torah, the Anunnaki of Nibiru.

Those signs include the visions at Fatima, Portugal (see Michael Hesemann's 2000 paperback book, *The Fatima Secret*, that explains the 'visions' as a UFO sighting), UFOs (including the abduction and breeding program; see works by researchers and writers such as Fowler, Jacobs, Mack, Strieber, and Hopkins), and crop circles.

Also, all periods of Jewish persecution are encoded in the Torah (see my book featured on my website www.AlienEndofDays.com), and the winners and losers of <u>all</u> U.S. presidential races since 1789 through 2016 are encoded in the Torah – the winners ("elected USA president") "defeat" (encoded term with names) their opponents – shown at my website www.PredictingPresidents.com.

Alien Mystery #10: Who Made the Mars Structures at Cydonia, and Have They Returned There?

The massive architectural structures (Richard Hoagland calls them 'Monuments') at Cydonia were made, I have concluded, by the Anunnaki of Nibiru, about 400,000 years ago (Hoagland's estimate of their age; see his book *The Monuments of Mars*).

That they were designed and constructed by the Anunnaki can be deduced by assessing four bodies of corroborative evidence: (1) some of the same mathematical construction and geometrical layout constants and angle ratios are the same as used in some crop formations designs (see Hoagland's book, above). So those who make crop circles and made the Mars structures are the same beings.

(2) The Mars connection can be seen in crop circles that use a 'six-pointed star,' which is an ancient Sumerian symbol for Mars (see Sitchin's books on how they were taught by the Anunnaki to count planets from the outer parts of the solar system inward, thus making Mars the sixth planet in order from Pluto; yes, the Sumerians knew of <u>all</u> the planets, even their colors and relative sizes, as they recorded what they were taught by their teachers, the Anunnaki. Modern science history says that Pluto was not discovered until 1930, and the colors of the planets were not verified by NASA until the 1970s and 1980s.

(3) The Face on Mars, as explained by Sitchin in his 2002 book *The Lost Book of Enki*, is a portrait of **Alalu**, ex-king of Nibiru, in exile, who discovered gold on Earth, thus saving Nibiru's atmosphere and the planet from ecological disaster. He became a great hero. The mile-long carved portrait of him wearing his helmet is an immortal tribute to his importance in the history of Nibiru. The carved mountain also serves as his tomb, per Sitchin. His second exile was to Mars, his final resting place. All aspects of the Face are found encoded in the Torah (an Anunnaki-dictated document composed and encrypted by them). See my 615-page book, 8.5" x 11", featured at my website www.MartianGodsTorahCoeEvidence.com.

The Torah also encodes **all** aspects of the 1989 shoot-down in Mars orbit of the Russian space probe 'Phobos 2' – even identifying who manned the 'weapon' used to shoot it down. See same book featured at website above; book shows many Torah matrices illustrating all descriptive elements of the event, including "Russian craft," "1989," and "shootdown."

Fig. 25

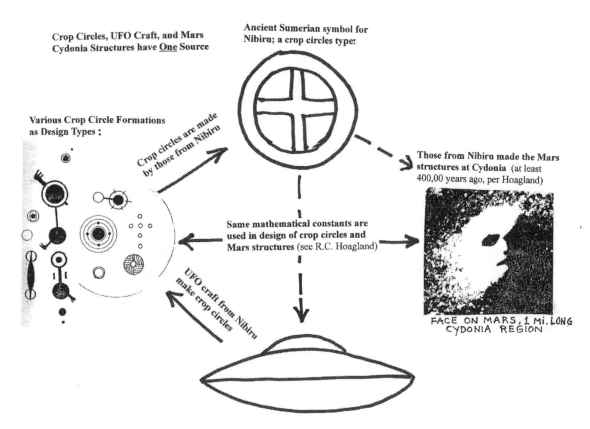

Crop Circles, UFO Craft, and Mars Cydonia Structures have <u>One</u> Source

Ancient Sumerian symbol for Nibiru; a crop circles type:

Various Crop Circle Formations as Design Types :

Crop circles are made by those from Nibiru

Those from Nibiru made the Mars structures at Cydonia (at least 400,00 years ago, per Hoagland)

Same mathematical constants are used in design of crop circles and Mars structures (see R.C. Hoagland)

UFO craft from Nibiru make crop circles

FACE ON MARS, 1 Mi. LONG CYDONIA REGION

ABOUT THE AUTHOR

Born in Maine in 1941, he was educated in 3 states and five countries, including later at Uppsala University, Sweden, and Alliance Francaise, Paris, France. He now lives deep in the California high desert, having retired early from a coastal county's Social Services department, and devotes himself full time to writing – dozens of books on how to decipher crop circles since 1990, and dozens of poems published in literary journals in 5 countries since 1968. He taught school (maths and science) at a private boys school in northern England 1967-68, and has degrees in Sociology. Divorced in 1975, San Francisco; no children.

He has conducted college and university extensions courses in Massachusetts and California 1988-1998, including on writing poetry; given public lectures on his crop circle decipherment findings and theory throughout California and in Tucson, Arizona; been interviewed on Fox-TV's "Encounters" (1995), and on TV affiliate in Santa Maria, California, cable access TV in Santa Barbara, and cable access in Tucson ("The Cutting Edge," in 2004 and 2005). Also interviewed for the History 2 channel in 2015, on his Bible Code findings, and interviewed on various radio shows (local, regional, and Canadian), including "Coast to Coast" in mid-December, 2000. Also on internet radio, Feb. 12, 2014.

More recently, his interest in Bible Codes has resulted in a series of dozens of self-published books. One of his websites, www.PredictingPresidents.com offers his book that explains how he discovered two Bible Code search result factors that can be used to predict with 100% accuracy the outcome of every U.S. presidential election throughout American history, and shows his original discovery as applied to every presidential election from 1789 to 2008 (as 'BHObama'). Elections in 2012 and 2016 are shown in other places and separately; 2016 as 'DJTrump elected USA president November 2016' found encoded in the Torah; November as the Hebrew month spelling, and 2016 and the Hebrew Calendar year 5777.

Printed in the United States
By Bookmasters